Mometrix
TEST PREPARATION

DSST®

Principles of Public Speaking Exam Secrets Study Guide

DEAR FUTURE EXAM SUCCESS STORY

First of all, **THANK YOU** for purchasing Mometrix study materials!

Second, congratulations! You are one of the few determined test-takers who are committed to doing whatever it takes to excel on your exam. **You have come to the right place.** We developed these study materials with one goal in mind: to deliver you the information you need in a format that's concise and easy to use.

In addition to optimizing your guide for the content of the test, we've outlined our recommended steps for breaking down the preparation process into small, attainable goals so you can make sure you stay on track.

We've also analyzed the entire test-taking process, identifying the most common pitfalls and showing how you can overcome them and be ready for any curveball the test throws you.

Standardized testing is one of the biggest obstacles on your road to success, which only increases the importance of doing well in the high-pressure, high-stakes environment of test day. Your results on this test could have a significant impact on your future, and this guide provides the information and practical advice to help you achieve your full potential on test day.

Your success is our success

We would love to hear from you! If you would like to share the story of your exam success or if you have any questions or comments in regard to our products, please contact us at **800-673-8175** or **support@mometrix.com**.

Thanks again for your business and we wish you continued success!

Sincerely,
The Mometrix Test Preparation Team

Written and edited by the Mometrix Exam Secrets Test Prep Team
Printed in the United States of America

TABLE OF CONTENTS

Introduction

Thank you for purchasing this resource! You have made the choice to prepare yourself for a test that could have a huge impact on your future, and this guide is designed to help you be fully ready for test day. Obviously, it's important to have a solid understanding of the test material, but you also need to be prepared for the unique environment and stressors of the test, so that you can perform to the best of your abilities.

For this purpose, the first section that appears in this guide is the **Secret Keys**. We've devoted countless hours to meticulously researching what works and what doesn't, and we've boiled down our findings to the five most impactful steps you can take to improve your performance on the test. We start at the beginning with study planning and move through the preparation process, all the way to the testing strategies that will help you get the most out of what you know when you're finally sitting in front of the test.

We recommend that you start preparing for your test as far in advance as possible. However, if you've bought this guide as a last-minute study resource and only have a few days before your test, we recommend that you skip over the first two Secret Keys since they address a long-term study plan.

If you struggle with **test anxiety**, we strongly encourage you to check out our recommendations for how you can overcome it. Test anxiety is a formidable foe, but it can be beaten, and we want to make sure you have the tools you need to defeat it.

Secret Key #1 – Plan Big, Study Small

There's a lot riding on your performance. If you want to ace this test, you're going to need to keep your skills sharp and the material fresh in your mind. You need a plan that lets you review everything you need to know while still fitting in your schedule. We'll break this strategy down into three categories.

Information Organization

Start with the information you already have: the official test outline. From this, you can make a complete list of all the concepts you need to cover before the test. Organize these concepts into groups that can be studied together, and create a list of any related vocabulary you need to learn so you can brush up on any difficult terms. You'll want to keep this vocabulary list handy once you actually start studying since you may need to add to it along the way.

Time Management

Once you have your set of study concepts, decide how to spread them out over the time you have left before the test. Break your study plan into small, clear goals so you have a manageable task for each day and know exactly what you're doing. Then just focus on one small step at a time. When you manage your time this way, you don't need to spend hours at a time studying. Studying a small block of content for a short period each day helps you retain information better and avoid stressing over how much you have left to do. You can relax knowing that you have a plan to cover everything in time. In order for this strategy to be effective though, you have to start studying early and stick to your schedule. Avoid the exhaustion and futility that comes from last-minute cramming!

Study Environment

The environment you study in has a big impact on your learning. Studying in a coffee shop, while probably more enjoyable, is not likely to be as fruitful as studying in a quiet room. It's important to keep distractions to a minimum. You're only planning to study for a short block of time, so make the most of it. Don't pause to check your phone or get up to find a snack. It's also important to **avoid multitasking**. Research has consistently shown that multitasking will make your studying dramatically less effective. Your study area should also be comfortable and well-lit so you don't have the distraction of straining your eyes or sitting on an uncomfortable chair.

The time of day you study is also important. You want to be rested and alert. Don't wait until just before bedtime. Study when you'll be most likely to comprehend and remember. Even better, if you know what time of day your test will be, set that time aside for study. That way your brain will be used to working on that subject at that specific time and you'll have a better chance of recalling information.

Finally, it can be helpful to team up with others who are studying for the same test. Your actual studying should be done in as isolated an environment as possible, but the work of organizing the information and setting up the study plan can be divided up. In between study sessions, you can discuss with your teammates the concepts that you're all studying and quiz each other on the details. Just be sure that your teammates are as serious about the test as you are. If you find that your study time is being replaced with social time, you might need to find a new team.

Secret Key #2 – Make Your Studying Count

You're devoting a lot of time and effort to preparing for this test, so you want to be absolutely certain it will pay off. This means doing more than just reading the content and hoping you can remember it on test day. It's important to make every minute of study count. There are two main areas you can focus on to make your studying count.

Retention

It doesn't matter how much time you study if you can't remember the material. You need to make sure you are retaining the concepts. To check your retention of the information you're learning, try recalling it at later times with minimal prompting. Try carrying around flashcards and glance at one or two from time to time or ask a friend who's also studying for the test to quiz you.

To enhance your retention, look for ways to put the information into practice so that you can apply it rather than simply recalling it. If you're using the information in practical ways, it will be much easier to remember. Similarly, it helps to solidify a concept in your mind if you're not only reading it to yourself but also explaining it to someone else. Ask a friend to let you teach them about a concept you're a little shaky on (or speak aloud to an imaginary audience if necessary). As you try to summarize, define, give examples, and answer your friend's questions, you'll understand the concepts better and they will stay with you longer. Finally, step back for a big picture view and ask yourself how each piece of information fits with the whole subject. When you link the different concepts together and see them working together as a whole, it's easier to remember the individual components.

Finally, practice showing your work on any multi-step problems, even if you're just studying. Writing out each step you take to solve a problem will help solidify the process in your mind, and you'll be more likely to remember it during the test.

Modality

Modality simply refers to the means or method by which you study. Choosing a study modality that fits your own individual learning style is crucial. No two people learn best in exactly the same way, so it's important to know your strengths and use them to your advantage.

For example, if you learn best by visualization, focus on visualizing a concept in your mind and draw an image or a diagram. Try color-coding your notes, illustrating them, or creating symbols that will trigger your mind to recall a learned concept. If you learn best by hearing or discussing information, find a study partner who learns the same way or read aloud to yourself. Think about how to put the information in your own words. Imagine that you are giving a lecture on the topic and record yourself so you can listen to it later.

For any learning style, flashcards can be helpful. Organize the information so you can take advantage of spare moments to review. Underline key words or phrases. Use different colors for different categories. Mnemonic devices (such as creating a short list in which every item starts with the same letter) can also help with retention. Find what works best for you and use it to store the information in your mind most effectively and easily.

Secret Key #3 – Practice the Right Way

Your success on test day depends not only on how many hours you put into preparing, but also on whether you prepared the right way. It's good to check along the way to see if your studying is paying off. One of the most effective ways to do this is by taking practice tests to evaluate your progress. Practice tests are useful because they show exactly where you need to improve. Every time you take a practice test, pay special attention to these three groups of questions:

- The questions you got wrong
- The questions you had to guess on, even if you guessed right
- The questions you found difficult or slow to work through

This will show you exactly what your weak areas are, and where you need to devote more study time. Ask yourself why each of these questions gave you trouble. Was it because you didn't understand the material? Was it because you didn't remember the vocabulary? Do you need more repetitions on this type of question to build speed and confidence? Dig into those questions and figure out how you can strengthen your weak areas as you go back to review the material.

Additionally, many practice tests have a section explaining the answer choices. It can be tempting to read the explanation and think that you now have a good understanding of the concept. However, an explanation likely only covers part of the question's broader context. Even if the explanation makes perfect sense, **go back and investigate** every concept related to the question until you're positive you have a thorough understanding.

As you go along, keep in mind that the practice test is just that: practice. Memorizing these questions and answers will not be very helpful on the actual test because it is unlikely to have any of the same exact questions. If you only know the right answers to the sample questions, you won't be prepared for the real thing. **Study the concepts** until you understand them fully, and then you'll be able to answer any question that shows up on the test.

It's important to wait on the practice tests until you're ready. If you take a test on your first day of study, you may be overwhelmed by the amount of material covered and how much you need to learn. Work up to it gradually.

On test day, you'll need to be prepared for answering questions, managing your time, and using the test-taking strategies you've learned. It's a lot to balance, like a mental marathon that will have a big impact on your future. Like training for a marathon, you'll need to start slowly and work your way up. When test day arrives, you'll be ready.

Start with the strategies you've read in the first two Secret Keys—plan your course and study in the way that works best for you. If you have time, consider using multiple study resources to get different approaches to the same concepts. It can be helpful to see difficult concepts from more than one angle. Then find a good source for practice tests. Many times, the test website will suggest potential study resources or provide sample tests.

Practice Test Strategy

If you're able to find at least three practice tests, we recommend this strategy:

Untimed and Open-Book Practice

Take the first test with no time constraints and with your notes and study guide handy. Take your time and focus on applying the strategies you've learned.

Timed and Open-Book Practice

Take the second practice test open-book as well, but set a timer and practice pacing yourself to finish in time.

Timed and Closed-Book Practice

Take any other practice tests as if it were test day. Set a timer and put away your study materials. Sit at a table or desk in a quiet room, imagine yourself at the testing center, and answer questions as quickly and accurately as possible.

Keep repeating timed and closed-book tests on a regular basis until you run out of practice tests or it's time for the actual test. Your mind will be ready for the schedule and stress of test day, and you'll be able to focus on recalling the material you've learned.

Secret Key #4 – Pace Yourself

Once you're fully prepared for the material on the test, your biggest challenge on test day will be managing your time. Just knowing that the clock is ticking can make you panic even if you have plenty of time left. Work on pacing yourself so you can build confidence against the time constraints of the exam. Pacing is a difficult skill to master, especially in a high-pressure environment, so **practice is vital**.

Set time expectations for your pace based on how much time is available. For example, if a section has 60 questions and the time limit is 30 minutes, you know you have to average 30 seconds or less per question in order to answer them all. Although 30 seconds is the hard limit, set 25 seconds per question as your goal, so you reserve extra time to spend on harder questions. When you budget extra time for the harder questions, you no longer have any reason to stress when those questions take longer to answer.

Don't let this time expectation distract you from working through the test at a calm, steady pace, but keep it in mind so you don't spend too much time on any one question. Recognize that taking extra time on one question you don't understand may keep you from answering two that you do understand later in the test. If your time limit for a question is up and you're still not sure of the answer, mark it and move on, and come back to it later if the time and the test format allow. If the testing format doesn't allow you to return to earlier questions, just make an educated guess; then put it out of your mind and move on.

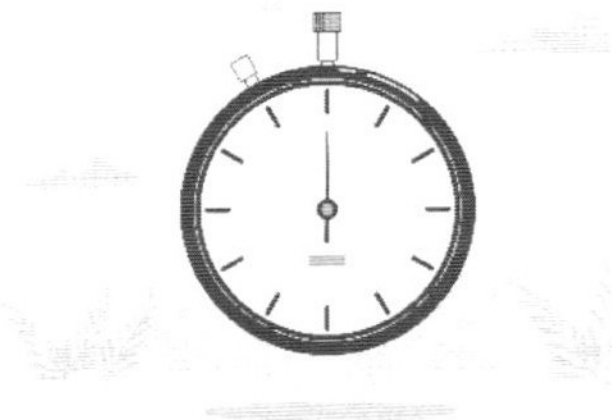

On the easier questions, be careful not to rush. It may seem wise to hurry through them so you have more time for the challenging ones, but it's not worth missing one if you know the concept and just didn't take the time to read the question fully. Work efficiently but make sure you understand the question and have looked at all of the answer choices, since more than one may seem right at first.

Even if you're paying attention to the time, you may find yourself a little behind at some point. You should speed up to get back on track, but do so wisely. Don't panic; just take a few seconds less on each question until you're caught up. Don't guess without thinking, but do look through the answer choices and eliminate any you know are wrong. If you can get down to two choices, it is often worthwhile to guess from those. Once you've chosen an answer, move on and don't dwell on any that you skipped or had to hurry through. If a question was taking too long, chances are it was one of the harder ones, so you weren't as likely to get it right anyway.

On the other hand, if you find yourself getting ahead of schedule, it may be beneficial to slow down a little. The more quickly you work, the more likely you are to make a careless mistake that will affect your score. You've budgeted time for each question, so don't be afraid to spend that time. Practice an efficient but careful pace to get the most out of the time you have.

Secret Key #5 – Have a Plan for Guessing

When you're taking the test, you may find yourself stuck on a question. Some of the answer choices seem better than others, but you don't see the one answer choice that is obviously correct. What do you do?

The scenario described above is very common, yet most test takers have not effectively prepared for it. Developing and practicing a plan for guessing may be one of the single most effective uses of your time as you get ready for the exam.

In developing your plan for guessing, there are three questions to address:

- When should you start the guessing process?
- How should you narrow down the choices?
- Which answer should you choose?

When to Start the Guessing Process

Unless your plan for guessing is to select C every time (which, despite its merits, is not what we recommend), you need to leave yourself enough time to apply your answer elimination strategies. Since you have a limited amount of time for each question, that means that if you're going to give yourself the best shot at guessing correctly, you have to decide quickly whether or not you will guess.

Of course, the best-case scenario is that you don't have to guess at all, so first, see if you can answer the question based on your knowledge of the subject and basic reasoning skills. Focus on the key words in the question and try to jog your memory of related topics. Give yourself a chance to bring the knowledge to mind, but once you realize that you don't have (or you can't access) the knowledge you need to answer the question, it's time to start the guessing process.

It's almost always better to start the guessing process too early than too late. It only takes a few seconds to remember something and answer the question from knowledge. Carefully eliminating wrong answer choices takes longer. Plus, going through the process of eliminating answer choices can actually help jog your memory.

Summary: Start the guessing process as soon as you decide that you can't answer the question based on your knowledge.

How to Narrow Down the Choices

The next chapter in this book (**Test-Taking Strategies**) includes a wide range of strategies for how to approach questions and how to look for answer choices to eliminate. You will definitely want to read those carefully, practice them, and figure out which ones work best for you. Here though, we're going to address a mindset rather than a particular strategy.

Your odds of guessing an answer correctly depend on how many options you are choosing from.

Number of options left	5	4	3	2	1
Odds of guessing correctly	20%	25%	33%	50%	100%

You can see from this chart just how valuable it is to be able to eliminate incorrect answers and make an educated guess, but there are two things that many test takers do that cause them to miss out on the benefits of guessing:

- Accidentally eliminating the correct answer
- Selecting an answer based on an impression

We'll look at the first one here, and the second one in the next section.

To avoid accidentally eliminating the correct answer, we recommend a thought exercise called **the $5 challenge**. In this challenge, you only eliminate an answer choice from contention if you are willing to bet $5 on it being wrong. Why $5? Five dollars is a small but not insignificant amount of money. It's an amount you could afford to lose but wouldn't want to throw away. And while losing $5 once might not hurt too much, doing it twenty times will set you back $100. In the same way, each small decision you make—eliminating a choice here, guessing on a question there—won't by itself impact your score very much, but when you put them all together, they can make a big difference. By holding each answer choice elimination decision to a higher standard, you can reduce the risk of accidentally eliminating the correct answer.

The $5 challenge can also be applied in a positive sense: If you are willing to bet $5 that an answer choice *is* correct, go ahead and mark it as correct.

Summary: Only eliminate an answer choice if you are willing to bet $5 that it is wrong.

Which Answer to Choose

You're taking the test. You've run into a hard question and decided you'll have to guess. You've eliminated all the answer choices you're willing to bet $5 on. Now you have to pick an answer. Why do we even need to talk about this? Why can't you just pick whichever one you feel like when the time comes?

The answer to these questions is that if you don't come into the test with a plan, you'll rely on your impression to select an answer choice, and if you do that, you risk falling into a trap. The test writers know that everyone who takes their test will be guessing on some of the questions, so they intentionally write wrong answer choices to seem plausible. You still have to pick an answer though, and if the wrong answer choices are designed to look right, how can you ever be sure that you're not falling for their trap? The best solution we've found to this dilemma is to take the decision out of your hands entirely. Here is the process we recommend:

Once you've eliminated any choices that you are confident (willing to bet $5) are wrong, select the first remaining choice as your answer.

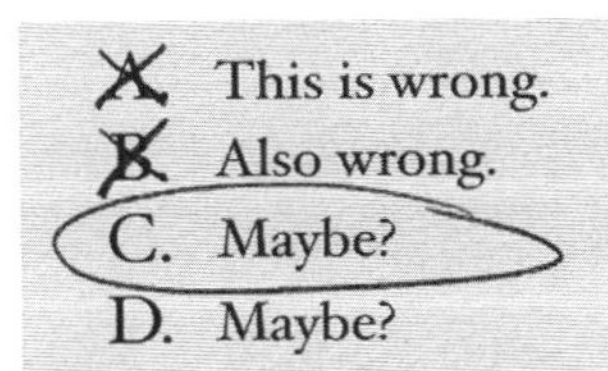

Whether you choose to select the first remaining choice, the second, or the last, the important thing is that you use some preselected standard. Using this approach guarantees that you will not be enticed into selecting an answer choice that looks right, because you are not basing your decision on how the answer choices look.

This is not meant to make you question your knowledge. Instead, it is to help you recognize the difference between your knowledge and your impressions. There's a huge difference between thinking an answer is right because of what you know, and thinking an answer is right because it looks or sounds like it should be right.

Summary: To ensure that your selection is appropriately random, make a predetermined selection from among all answer choices you have not eliminated.

Test-Taking Strategies

This section contains a list of test-taking strategies that you may find helpful as you work through the test. By taking what you know and applying logical thought, you can maximize your chances of answering any question correctly!

It is very important to realize that every question is different and every person is different: no single strategy will work on every question, and no single strategy will work for every person. That's why we've included all of them here, so you can try them out and determine which ones work best for different types of questions and which ones work best for you.

Question Strategies

✓ Read Carefully

Read the question and the answer choices carefully. Don't miss the question because you misread the terms. You have plenty of time to read each question thoroughly and make sure you understand what is being asked. Yet a happy medium must be attained, so don't waste too much time. You must read carefully and efficiently.

✓ Contextual Clues

Look for contextual clues. If the question includes a word you are not familiar with, look at the immediate context for some indication of what the word might mean. Contextual clues can often give you all the information you need to decipher the meaning of an unfamiliar word. Even if you can't determine the meaning, you may be able to narrow down the possibilities enough to make a solid guess at the answer to the question.

✓ Prefixes

If you're having trouble with a word in the question or answer choices, try dissecting it. Take advantage of every clue that the word might include. Prefixes can be a huge help. Usually, they allow you to determine a basic meaning. *Pre-* means before, *post-* means after, *pro-* is positive, *de-* is negative. From prefixes, you can get an idea of the general meaning of the word and try to put it into context.

✓ Hedge Words

Watch out for critical hedge words, such as *likely, may, can, often, almost, mostly, usually, generally, rarely,* and *sometimes*. Question writers insert these hedge phrases to cover every possibility. Often an answer choice will be wrong simply because it leaves no room for exception. Be on guard for answer choices that have definitive words such as *exactly* and *always.*

✓ Switchback Words

Stay alert for *switchbacks*. These are the words and phrases frequently used to alert you to shifts in thought. The most common switchback words are *but, although,* and *however*. Others include *nevertheless, on the other hand, even though, while, in spite of, despite,* and *regardless of*. Switchback words are important to catch because they can change the direction of the question or an answer choice.

☑ FACE VALUE

When in doubt, use common sense. Accept the situation in the problem at face value. Don't read too much into it. These problems will not require you to make wild assumptions. If you have to go beyond creativity and warp time or space in order to have an answer choice fit the question, then you should move on and consider the other answer choices. These are normal problems rooted in reality. The applicable relationship or explanation may not be readily apparent, but it is there for you to figure out. Use your common sense to interpret anything that isn't clear.

Answer Choice Strategies

☑ ANSWER SELECTION

The most thorough way to pick an answer choice is to identify and eliminate wrong answers until only one is left, then confirm it is the correct answer. Sometimes an answer choice may immediately seem right, but be careful. The test writers will usually put more than one reasonable answer choice on each question, so take a second to read all of them and make sure that the other choices are not equally obvious. As long as you have time left, it is better to read every answer choice than to pick the first one that looks right without checking the others.

☑ ANSWER CHOICE FAMILIES

An answer choice family consists of two (in rare cases, three) answer choices that are very similar in construction and cannot all be true at the same time. If you see two answer choices that are direct opposites or parallels, one of them is usually the correct answer. For instance, if one answer choice says that quantity *x* increases and another either says that quantity *x* decreases (opposite) or says that quantity *y* increases (parallel), then those answer choices would fall into the same family. An answer choice that doesn't match the construction of the answer choice family is more likely to be incorrect. Most questions will not have answer choice families, but when they do appear, you should be prepared to recognize them.

☑ ELIMINATE ANSWERS

Eliminate answer choices as soon as you realize they are wrong, but make sure you consider all possibilities. If you are eliminating answer choices and realize that the last one you are left with is also wrong, don't panic. Start over and consider each choice again. There may be something you missed the first time that you will realize on the second pass.

☑ AVOID FACT TRAPS

Don't be distracted by an answer choice that is factually true but doesn't answer the question. You are looking for the choice that answers the question. Stay focused on what the question is asking for so you don't accidentally pick an answer that is true but incorrect. Always go back to the question and make sure the answer choice you've selected actually answers the question and is not merely a true statement.

☑ EXTREME STATEMENTS

In general, you should avoid answers that put forth extreme actions as standard practice or proclaim controversial ideas as established fact. An answer choice that states the "process should be used in certain situations, if…" is much more likely to be correct than one that states the "process should be discontinued completely." The first is a calm rational statement and doesn't even make a definitive, uncompromising stance, using a hedge word *if* to provide wiggle room, whereas the second choice is far more extreme.

⊘ BENCHMARK

As you read through the answer choices and you come across one that seems to answer the question well, mentally select that answer choice. This is not your final answer, but it's the one that will help you evaluate the other answer choices. The one that you selected is your benchmark or standard for judging each of the other answer choices. Every other answer choice must be compared to your benchmark. That choice is correct until proven otherwise by another answer choice beating it. If you find a better answer, then that one becomes your new benchmark. Once you've decided that no other choice answers the question as well as your benchmark, you have your final answer.

⊘ PREDICT THE ANSWER

Before you even start looking at the answer choices, it is often best to try to predict the answer. When you come up with the answer on your own, it is easier to avoid distractions and traps because you will know exactly what to look for. The right answer choice is unlikely to be word-for-word what you came up with, but it should be a close match. Even if you are confident that you have the right answer, you should still take the time to read each option before moving on.

General Strategies

⊘ TOUGH QUESTIONS

If you are stumped on a problem or it appears too hard or too difficult, don't waste time. Move on! Remember though, if you can quickly check for obviously incorrect answer choices, your chances of guessing correctly are greatly improved. Before you completely give up, at least try to knock out a couple of possible answers. Eliminate what you can and then guess at the remaining answer choices before moving on.

⊘ CHECK YOUR WORK

Since you will probably not know every term listed and the answer to every question, it is important that you get credit for the ones that you do know. Don't miss any questions through careless mistakes. If at all possible, try to take a second to look back over your answer selection and make sure you've selected the correct answer choice and haven't made a costly careless mistake (such as marking an answer choice that you didn't mean to mark). This quick double check should more than pay for itself in caught mistakes for the time it costs.

⊘ PACE YOURSELF

It's easy to be overwhelmed when you're looking at a page full of questions; your mind is confused and full of random thoughts, and the clock is ticking down faster than you would like. Calm down and maintain the pace that you have set for yourself. Especially as you get down to the last few minutes of the test, don't let the small numbers on the clock make you panic. As long as you are on track by monitoring your pace, you are guaranteed to have time for each question.

⊘ DON'T RUSH

It is very easy to make errors when you are in a hurry. Maintaining a fast pace in answering questions is pointless if it makes you miss questions that you would have gotten right otherwise. Test writers like to include distracting information and wrong answers that seem right. Taking a little extra time to avoid careless mistakes can make all the difference in your test score. Find a pace that allows you to be confident in the answers that you select.

⊘ Keep Moving

Panicking will not help you pass the test, so do your best to stay calm and keep moving. Taking deep breaths and going through the answer elimination steps you practiced can help to break through a stress barrier and keep your pace.

Final Notes

The combination of a solid foundation of content knowledge and the confidence that comes from practicing your plan for applying that knowledge is the key to maximizing your performance on test day. As your foundation of content knowledge is built up and strengthened, you'll find that the strategies included in this chapter become more and more effective in helping you quickly sift through the distractions and traps of the test to isolate the correct answer.

Now that you're preparing to move forward into the test content chapters of this book, be sure to keep your goal in mind. As you read, think about how you will be able to apply this information on the test. If you've already seen sample questions for the test and you have an idea of the question format and style, try to come up with questions of your own that you can answer based on what you're reading. This will give you valuable practice applying your knowledge in the same ways you can expect to on test day.

Good luck and good studying!

Principles of Public Speaking

Outlining and Organizing Ideas

Main Ideas, Supporting Details, and Outlining a Topic

A writer often begins the first paragraph of a paper by stating the **main idea** or point, also known as the **topic sentence**. The rest of the paragraph supplies particular details that develop and support the main point. One way to visualize the relationship between the main point and supporting information is as a table: the tabletop is the main point, and each of the table's legs is a supporting detail or group of details. Both professional authors and students can benefit from planning their writing by first making an outline of the topic. Outlines facilitate quick identification of the main point and supporting details without having to wade through the additional language that will exist in the fully developed essay, article, or paper. Outlining can also help readers to analyze a piece of existing writing for the same reason. The outline first summarizes the main idea in one sentence. Then, below that, it summarizes the supporting details in a numbered list. Writing the paper then consists of filling in the outline with detail, writing a paragraph for each supporting point, and adding an introduction and conclusion.

Introduction

The purpose of the introduction is to capture the reader's attention and announce the essay's main idea. Normally, the introduction contains 50-80 words, or 3-5 sentences. An introduction can begin with an interesting quote, a question, or a strong opinion—something that will **engage** the reader's interest and prompt them to keep reading. If you are writing your essay to a specific prompt, your introduction should include a **restatement or summarization** of the prompt so that the reader will have some context for your essay. Finally, your introduction should briefly state your **thesis or main idea**: the primary thing you hope to communicate to the reader through your essay. Don't try to include all of the details and nuances of your thesis, or all of your reasons for it, in the introduction. That's what the rest of the essay is for!

Review Video: Introduction
Visit mometrix.com/academy and enter code: 961328

Thesis Statement

The thesis is the main idea of the essay. A temporary thesis should be established early in the writing process because it will serve to keep the writer focused as ideas develop. This temporary thesis is subject to change as you continue to write.

The temporary thesis has two parts: a topic (i.e., the focus of your essay based on the prompt) and a comment. The comment makes an important point about the topic. A temporary thesis should be interesting and specific. Also, you need to limit the topic to a manageable scope. These three criteria are useful tools to measure the effectiveness of any temporary thesis:

- Does the focus of my essay have enough interest to hold an audience?
- Is the focus of my essay specific enough to generate interest?
- Is the focus of my essay manageable for the time limit? Too broad? Too narrow?

The thesis should be a generalization rather than a fact because the thesis prepares readers for facts and details that support the thesis. The process of bringing the thesis into sharp focus may help in outlining major sections of the work. Once the thesis and introduction are complete, you can address the body of the work.

Review Video: Thesis Statements
Visit mometrix.com/academy and enter code: 691033

Supporting the Thesis

Throughout your essay, the thesis should be **explained clearly and supported** adequately by additional arguments. The thesis sentence needs to contain a clear statement of the purpose of your essay and a comment about the thesis. With the thesis statement, you have an opportunity to state what is noteworthy of this particular treatment of the prompt. Each sentence and paragraph should build on and support the thesis.

When you respond to the prompt, use parts of the passage to support your argument or defend your position. With supporting evidence from the passage, you strengthen your argument because readers can see your attention to the entire passage and your response to the details and facts within the passage. You can use facts, details, statistics, and direct quotations from the passage to uphold your position. Be sure to point out which information comes from the original passage and base your argument around that evidence.

Body

In an essay's introduction, the writer establishes the thesis and may indicate how the rest of the piece will be structured. In the body of the piece, the writer **elaborates** upon, **illustrates**, and **explains** the **thesis statement**. How writers sequence supporting details and their choices of paragraph types are development techniques. Writers may give examples of the concept introduced in the thesis statement. If the subject includes a cause-and-effect relationship, the author may explain its causality. A writer will explain and/or analyze the main idea of the piece throughout the body, often by presenting arguments for the veracity or credibility of the thesis statement. Writers may use development to define or clarify ambiguous terms. Paragraphs within the body may be organized with natural sequences, like space and time. Writers may employ **inductive reasoning**, using multiple details to establish a generalization or causal relationship, or **deductive reasoning**, proving a generalized hypothesis or proposition through a specific example/case.

Review Video: Drafting Body Paragraphs
Visit mometrix.com/academy and enter code: 724590

Paragraphs

After the introduction of a passage, a series of body paragraphs will carry a message through to the conclusion. A paragraph should be **unified around a main point**. Normally, a good topic sentence summarizes the paragraph's main point. A topic sentence is a general sentence that gives an introduction to the paragraph.

The sentences that follow support the topic sentence. However, the topic sentence can come as the final sentence to the paragraph if the earlier sentences give a clear explanation of the topic sentence. Overall, the paragraphs need to stay true to the main point. This means that any unnecessary sentences that do not advance the main point should be removed.

The main point of a paragraph requires adequate development (i.e., a substantial paragraph that covers the main point). A paragraph of two or three sentences does not cover a main point. This is true when the main point of the paragraph gives strong support to the argument of the thesis. An occasional short paragraph is fine as a transitional device. However, a well-developed argument will have paragraphs with more than a few sentences.

Methods of Developing Paragraphs

Common methods of adding substance to paragraphs include examples, illustrations, analogies, and cause and effect.

- **Examples** are the supporting details to the main idea of a paragraph or a passage. When authors write about something that their audience may not understand, they can provide an example to show their point. When authors write about something that is not easily accepted, they can give examples to prove their point.
- **Illustrations** are extended examples that require several sentences. Well selected illustrations can be a great way for authors to develop a point that may not be familiar to their audience.
- **Analogies** make comparisons between items that appear to have nothing in common. Analogies are employed by writers to provoke fresh thoughts about a subject. These comparisons may be used to explain the unfamiliar, to clarify an abstract point, or to argue a point. Although analogies are effective literary devices, they should be used carefully in arguments. Two things may be alike in some respects but completely different in others.
- **Cause and effect** is an excellent device used when the cause and effect are accepted as true. One way that authors can use cause and effect is to state the effect in the topic sentence of a paragraph and add the causes in the body of the paragraph. With this method, an author's paragraphs can have structure which always strengthens writing.

Review Video: How to Write a Good Paragraph
Visit mometrix.com/academy and enter code: 682127

Types of Paragraphs

A **paragraph of narration** tells a story or a part of a story. Normally, the sentences are arranged in chronological order (i.e., the order that the events happened). However, flashbacks (i.e., an anecdote from an earlier time) can be included.

A **descriptive paragraph** makes a verbal portrait of a person, place, or thing. When specific details are used that appeal to one or more of the senses (i.e., sight, sound, smell, taste, and touch), authors give readers a sense of being present in the moment.

A **process paragraph** is related to time order (i.e., First, you open the bottle. Second, you pour the liquid, etc.). Usually, this describes a process or teaches readers how to perform a process.

Comparing two things draws attention to their similarities and indicates a number of differences. When authors contrast, they focus only on differences. Both comparing and contrasting may be done point-by-point, noting both the similarities and differences of each point, or in sequential paragraphs, where you discuss the all the similarities and then all the differences, or vice versa.

Breaking Text into Paragraphs

For most forms of writing, you will need to use multiple paragraphs. As such, determining when to start a new paragraph is very important. Reasons for starting a new paragraph include:

1. To mark off the introduction and concluding paragraphs
2. To signal a shift to a new idea or topic
3. To indicate an important shift in time or place

4. To explain a point in additional detail
5. To highlight a comparison, contrast, or cause and effect relationship

Paragraph Length

Most readers find that their comfort level for a paragraph is between 100 and 200 words. Shorter paragraphs cause too much starting and stopping, and give a choppy effect. Paragraphs that are too long often test the attention span of readers. Two notable exceptions to this rule exist. In scientific or scholarly papers, longer paragraphs suggest seriousness and depth. In journalistic writing, constraints are placed on paragraph size by the narrow columns in a newspaper format.

The first and last paragraphs of a text will usually be the introduction and conclusion. These special-purpose paragraphs are likely to be shorter than paragraphs in the body of the work. Paragraphs in the body of the essay follow the subject's outline; one paragraph per point in short essays and a group of paragraphs per point in longer works. Some ideas require more development than others, so it is good for a writer to remain flexible. A paragraph of excessive length may be divided, and shorter ones may be combined.

Coherent Paragraphs

A smooth flow of sentences and paragraphs without gaps, shifts, or bumps will lead to paragraph coherence. Ties between old and new information can be smoothed by several methods:

- Linking ideas clearly, from the topic sentence to the body of the paragraph, is essential for a smooth transition. The topic sentence states the main point, and this should be followed by specific details, examples, and illustrations that support the topic sentence. The support may be direct or indirect. In indirect support, the illustrations and examples may support a sentence that in turn supports the topic directly.
- The repetition of key words adds coherence to a paragraph. To avoid dull language, variations of the key words may be used.
- Parallel structures are often used within sentences to emphasize the similarity of ideas and connect sentences giving similar information.
- Maintaining a consistent verb tense throughout the paragraph helps. Shifting tenses affects the smooth flow of words and can disrupt the coherence of the paragraph.

Sequence Words and Phrases

When a paragraph opens with the topic sentence, the second sentence may begin with a phrase like "First of all," introducing the first supporting detail/example. The writer may introduce the second supporting item with words or phrases like "Also," "In addition," and "Besides." The writer might introduce succeeding pieces of support with wording like, "Another thing," "Moreover" "Furthermore," or "Not only that, but." The writer may introduce the last piece of support with "Lastly," "Finally," or "Last but not least." Writers get off the point by presenting "off-target" items not supporting the main point. For example, a main point "My dog is not smart" is supported by the statement, "He's six years old and still doesn't answer to his name." But "He cries when I leave for school" is not supportive, as it does not indicate lack of intelligence. Writers stay on point by presenting only supportive statements that are directly relevant to and illustrative of their main point.

Transitions

Transitions between sentences and paragraphs guide readers from idea to idea. They also indicate relationships between sentences and paragraphs. Writers should be judicious in their use of transitions, inserting them sparingly. They should also be selected to fit the author's purpose—transitions can indicate time, comparison, and conclusion, among other purposes.

Review Video: Transitions in Writing
Visit mometrix.com/academy and enter code: 233246

Types of Transitional Words

Time	Afterward, immediately, earlier, meanwhile, recently, lately, now, since, soon, when, then, until, before, etc.
Sequence	too, first, second, further, moreover, also, again, and, next, still, too, besides, and finally
Comparison	similarly, in the same way, likewise, also, again, and once more
Contrasting	but, although, despite, however, instead, nevertheless, on the one hand... on the other hand, regardless, yet, and in contrast
Cause and Effect	because, consequently, thus, therefore, then, to this end, since, so, as a result, if... then, and accordingly
Examples	for example, for instance, such as, to illustrate, indeed, in fact, and specifically
Place	near, far, here, there, to the left/right, next to, above, below, beyond, opposite, and beside
Concession	granted that, naturally, of course, it may appear, and although it is true that
Repetition, Summary, or Conclusion	as mentioned earlier, as noted, in other words, in short, on the whole, to summarize, therefore, as a result, to conclude, and in conclusion

Conclusion

Two important principles to consider when writing a conclusion are strength and closure. A strong conclusion gives the reader a sense that the author's main points are meaningful and important, and that the supporting facts and arguments are convincing, solid, and well developed. When a conclusion achieves closure, it gives the impression that the writer has stated what needed stating and completed the work, rather than simply stopping after a specified length. Some things to avoid when writing concluding paragraphs include: introducing a completely new idea, beginning with obvious or unoriginal phrases like "In conclusion" or "To summarize," apologizing for one's opinions or writing, repeating the thesis word for word rather than rephrasing it, and believing that the conclusion must always summarize the piece.

Style and Form

Writing Style and Linguistic Form

Linguistic form encodes the literal meanings of words and sentences. It comes from the phonological, morphological, syntactic, and semantic parts of a language. **Writing style** consists of different ways of encoding the meaning and indicating figurative and stylistic meanings. An author's writing style can also be referred to as his or her **voice**.

Writers' stylistic choices accomplish three basic effects on their audiences:

- They **communicate meanings** beyond linguistically dictated meanings,
- They communicate the **author's attitude**, such as persuasive/argumentative effects accomplished through style, and
- They communicate or **express feelings**.

Within style, component areas include: narrative structure; viewpoint; focus; sound patterns; meter and rhythm; lexical and syntactic repetition and parallelism; writing genre; representational, realistic, and mimetic effects; representation of thought and speech; meta-representation (representing representation); irony; metaphor and other indirect meanings; representation and use of historical and dialectal variations; gender-specific and other group-specific speech styles, both real and fictitious; and analysis of the processes for inferring meaning from writing.

Level of Formality

The relationship between writer and reader is important in choosing a **level of formality** as most writing requires some degree of formality. **Formal writing** is for addressing a superior in a school or work environment. Business letters, textbooks, and newspapers use a moderate to high level of formality. **Informal writing** is appropriate for private letters, personal e-mails, and business correspondence between close associates.

For your exam, you will want to be aware of informal and formal writing. One way that this can be accomplished is to watch for shifts in point of view in the essay. For example, unless writers are using a personal example, they will rarely refer to themselves (e.g., "*I* think that *my* point is very clear.") to avoid being informal when they need to be formal.

Also, be mindful of an author who addresses his or her audience **directly** in their writing (e.g., "Readers, *like you*, will understand this argument.") as this can be a sign of informal writing. Good writers understand the need to be consistent with their level of formality. Shifts in levels of formality or point of view can confuse readers and cause them to discount the message.

Clichés

Clichés are phrases that have been **overused** to the point that the phrase has no importance or has lost the original meaning. These phrases have no originality and add very little to a passage. Therefore, most writers will avoid the use of clichés. Another option is to make changes to a cliché so that it is not predictable and empty of meaning.

Examples:

> When life gives you lemons, make lemonade.
>
> Every cloud has a silver lining.

Jargon

Jargon is a **specialized vocabulary** that is used among members of a trade or profession. Since jargon is understood by only a small audience, writers will use jargon in passages that will only be read by a specialized audience. For example, medical jargon should be used in a medical journal but not in a New York Times article. Jargon includes exaggerated language that tries to impress rather than inform. Sentences filled with jargon are not precise and are difficult to understand.

Examples:

> "He is going to *toenail* these frames for us." (Toenail is construction jargon for nailing at an angle.)
>
> "They brought in a *kip* of material today." (Kip refers to 1000 pounds in architecture and engineering.)

Slang

Slang is an **informal** and sometimes private language that is understood by some individuals. Slang has some usefulness, but the language can have a small audience. So, most formal writing will not include this kind of language.

Examples:

> "Yes, the event was a blast!" (In this sentence, *blast* means that the event was a great experience.)
>
> "That attempt was an epic fail." (By *epic fail*, the speaker means that his or her attempt was not a success.)

Colloquialism

A colloquialism is a word or phrase that is found in informal writing. Unlike slang, **colloquial language** will be familiar to a greater range of people. Colloquial language can include some slang, but these are limited to contractions for the most part.

Examples:

> "Can *y'all* come back another time?" (Y'all is a contraction of "you all" which has become a colloquialism.)
>
> "Will you stop him from building this *castle in the air*?" (A "castle in the air" is an improbable or unlikely event.)

Tone

Tone may be defined as the writer's **attitude** toward the topic, and to the audience. This attitude is reflected in the language used in the writing. The tone of a work should be **appropriate to the topic** and to the intended audience. Some texts should not contain slang or jargon, although these may be fine in a different piece. Tone can range from humorous to serious and all levels in between. It may be more or less formal, depending on the purpose of the writing and its intended audience. All these nuances in tone can flavor the entire writing and should be kept in mind as the work evolves.

Word Selection

A writer's choice of words is a **signature** of their style. Careful thought about the use of words can improve a piece of writing. A passage can be an exciting piece to read when attention is given to the use of vivid or specific nouns rather than general ones.

Example:

General: His kindness will never be forgotten.

Specific: His thoughtful gifts and bear hugs will never be forgotten.

Attention should also be given to the kind of verbs that are used in sentences. Active verbs (e.g., run, swim) should be about an action. Whenever possible, an **active verb should replace a linking verb** to provide clear examples for arguments and to strengthen a passage overall. When using an active verb, one should be sure that the verb is used in the active voice instead of the passive voice. Verbs are in the active voice when the subject is the one doing the action. A verb is in the passive voice when the subject is the recipient of an action.

Example:

Passive: The winners were called to the stage by the judges.

Active: The judges called the winners to the stage.

Review Video: Word Usage in Sentences
Visit mometrix.com/academy and enter code: 197863

CONCISENESS

Conciseness is writing what you need to get your message across in the fewest words possible. Planning is important in writing concise messages. If you have in mind what you need to write beforehand, it will be easier to make a message short and to the point. Do not state the obvious.

Revising is also important. After the message is written, make sure you have short sentences. When reviewing the information, imagine a conversation taking place, and concise writing will likely result.

TRANSITIONS

Transitions are bridges between what has been read and what is about to be read. Transitions smooth the reader's path between sentences and inform the reader of major connections to new ideas forthcoming in the text. Transitional phrases should be used with care, selecting the appropriate phrase for a transition. Tone is another important consideration in using transitional phrases, varying the tone for different audiences. For example, in a scholarly essay, *in summary* would be preferable to the more informal *in short.*

When working with transitional words and phrases, writers usually find a natural flow that indicates when a transition is needed. In reading a draft of the text, it should become apparent where the flow is uneven or rough. At this point, the writer can add transitional elements during the revision process. Revising can also afford an opportunity to delete transitional devices that seem heavy handed or unnecessary.

TYPES OF TRANSITIONS

Appropriate transition words help clarify the relationships between sentences and paragraphs, and they create a much more cohesive essay. Below are listed several categories of transitions that you will need to be familiar with, along with some associated transition words:

- **Logical Continuation**: therefore, as such, for this reason, thus, consequently, as a result
- **Extended Argument**: moreover, furthermore, also

- **Example or Illustration**: for instance, for example
- **Comparison**: similarly, likewise, in like manner
- **Contrast**: however, nevertheless, by contrast
- **Restatement or Clarification**: in other words, to put it another way
- **Generalization or General Application**: in broad terms, broadly speaking, in general

Review Video: Transition Words
Visit mometrix.com/academy and enter code: 707563

Rhetorical Devices

Rhetorical Devices

There are many types of language devices that authors use to convey their meaning in a descriptive way. Understanding these concepts will help you understand what you read. These types of devices are called **figurative language**—language that goes beyond the literal meaning of a word or phrase. **Descriptive language** specifically evokes imagery in the reader's mind to make a story come alive. **Exaggeration** is a type of figurative language in which an author carries an idea beyond the truth in order to emphasize something. A **simile** is a type of figurative language that compares two things that are not actually alike, using words such as *like* and *as*. A **metaphor** takes the comparison one step further by fully equating the two things rather than just saying they are similar.

A **figure-of-speech** is a word or phrase that departs from straightforward, literal language. Figures-of-speech are often used and crafted for emphasis, freshness of expression, or clarity. However, clarity of a passage may suffer from use of these devices. As an example of the figurative use of a word, consider the sentence: *I am going to crown you.* The author may mean:

- I am going to place a literal crown on your head.
- I am going to symbolically exalt you to the place of kingship.
- I am going to punch you in the head with my clenched fist.
- I am going to put a second checker piece on top of your checker piece to signify that it has become a king.

Review Video: Figures of Speech
Visit mometrix.com/academy and enter code: 111295

A **metaphor** is a type of figurative language in which the writer equates something with another thing that is not particularly similar. For instance, *the bird was an arrow arcing through the sky*. In this sentence, the arrow is serving as a metaphor for the bird. The point of a metaphor is to encourage the reader to consider the item being described in a *different way*. Let's continue with this metaphor for a bird. You are asked to envision the bird's flight as being similar to the arc of an arrow. So, you imagine the flight to be swift and bending. Metaphors are a way for the author to describe an item *without being direct and obvious*. This literary device is a lyrical and suggestive way of providing information. Note that the reference for a metaphor will not always be mentioned explicitly by the author. Consider the following description of a forest in winter: *Swaying skeletons reached for the sky and groaned as the wind blew through them.* In this example, the author is using *skeletons* as a metaphor for leafless trees. This metaphor creates a spooky tone while inspiring the reader's imagination.

Review Video: Metaphors in Writing
Visit mometrix.com/academy and enter code: 133295

A **simile** is a figurative expression that is similar to a metaphor, but the expression uses a distancing word: *like* or *as*. Examples include phrases such as *the sun was like an orange, eager as a beaver*, and *nimble as a mountain goat*. Because a simile includes *like* or *as,* the device creates more space between the description and the thing being described than a metaphor does. If an author says that *a house was like a shoebox*, then the tone is different than the author saying that the house *was* a shoebox. Authors will choose between a metaphor and a simile depending on their intended tone.

Review Video: Similes
Visit mometrix.com/academy and enter code: 642949

Another type of figurative language is **personification**. This is describing a nonhuman thing as if the item were human. Literally, the word means the process of making something into a person. The general intent of personification is to describe things in a manner that will be comprehensible to readers. When an author states that a tree *groans* in the wind, he or she does not mean that the tree is emitting a low, pained sound from a mouth. Instead, the author means that the tree is making a noise similar to a human groan. Of course, this personification establishes a tone of sadness or suffering. A different tone would be established if the author said that the tree was *swaying* or *dancing*.

Review Video: Personification
Visit mometrix.com/academy and enter code: 260066

Target Audience

Considerations to Teach Students About Occasions, Purposes, and Audiences

Teachers can explain to students that organizing their ideas, providing evidence to support the points they make in their writing, and correcting their grammar and mechanics are not simply for following writing rules or correctness for its own sake, but rather for ensuring that specific reader audiences understand what they intend to communicate. For example, upper-elementary-grade students writing for lower-elementary-grade students should write in print rather than script, use simpler vocabulary, and avoid writing in long, complex, compound, or complex-compound sentences. The purpose for writing guides word choice, such as encouraging readers to question opposing viewpoints or stimulate empathy and/or sympathy. It also influences narrative, descriptive, expository, or persuasive/argumentative format. For instance, business letters require different form and language than parent thank-you notes. Persuasive techniques, like words that evoke certain reader emotions, description that appeals to reader beliefs, and supporting information can all affect reader opinions.

Review Video: Writing Purpose and Audience
Visit mometrix.com/academy and enter code: 146627

Questions to Determine Content and Format

When student writers have chosen a viewpoint or idea about which to write, teachers can help them select content to include and the writing format most appropriate to their subject. They should have students ask themselves what their readers need to know to enable them to agree with the viewpoint in the writing, or to believe what the writer is saying. Students can imagine another person hearing them say what they will write about, and responding, "Oh, yeah? Prove that!" Teachers should have students ask themselves what kinds of evidence they need to prove their positions and ideas to skeptical readers. They should have students consider what points might cause the reader to disagree. Students should consider what knowledge their reading audience shares in common with them. They should also consider what information they need to share with their readers. Teachers can have students adapt various writing formats, organizing techniques, and writing styles to different purposes and audiences to practice choosing writing modes and language.

Appropriate Kinds of Writing for Different Tasks, Purposes, and Audiences

Students who are writing to persuade their parents to grant some additional privilege, such as permission for a more independent activity, should use more sophisticated vocabulary and diction that sounds more mature and serious to appeal to the parental audience. Students who are writing for younger children, however, should use simpler vocabulary and sentence structure, as well as choose words that are more vivid and entertaining. They should treat their topics more lightly, and include humor as appropriate. Students who are writing for their classmates may use language that is more informal, as well as age-appropriate. Students wanting to convince others to agree with them should use persuasive/argumentative form. Those wanting to share an experience should use descriptive writing. Those wanting to relate a story and what can be learned from it should write narratives. Students can use speculative writing to invite others to join them in exploring ideas.

Research

Research Writing

A research question or problem is what a researcher wants to answer or resolve. In a research paper, the problem statement clearly identifies the issue, tells why the researcher cares about this issue, defines the scope of the research by focusing on specific variables, and shows why those variables matter. The problem statement follows the title and abstract in the research paper, supplying context for the rest and getting the reader's attention. Whether professionals or students, when researchers conduct academic research projects, their literature reviews, which thoroughly examine the extant body of literature on their chosen research topic, form a necessary component of the project by showing what work has already been done toward answering the research question that they have chosen to investigate.

Addressing Research Questions

When asking a research question, the researcher may find through making a careful review of the existing literature that the question s/he has chosen have already been answered definitively. In this case, the researcher should modify the question or ask a different one. If the question has not been answered in the literature, researchers should consider the existing knowledge, the chronological sequence in which knowledge has been developed, whether there are any gaps in the knowledge, what needs and opportunities for additional research have been identified, and how one plans to fill in these gaps. Researchers should also consider whether consensus or controversy exists about pertinent matters and, with the latter, which positions exist. One should also consider research trajectories suggested by others' work and the most productive research direction indicated by the literature. Finally, researchers should realize there are no absolute answers: they must decide what is important in the context of their work.

Literature Review

One main part of a literature review is searching through existing literature. The other is actually writing the review. Researchers must take care not to get lost in the information without making any progress in their research goal. A good precaution is to write out the research question and keep it nearby. It is also wise to make a search plan and establish a time limit in advance. Finding a seemingly endless number of references indicates a need to revisit the research question because it is too broad. Finding too little material means that the research topic is too narrow. With cutting-edge research, one may find that nobody has investigated this particular question. This requires systematic searching, using abstracts in periodicals for an overview of available literature, research papers or other specific sources to explore its reference, and references in books and general sources.

When searching published literature on a research topic, one must take thorough notes. It is common to find a reference that could be useful later but is not needed now, so it is helpful to make a note of it so it will be easy to find later. These notes can be grouped in a word processing document, which also allows for easy compiling of links and quotes from Internet research. Researchers should connect to the Internet regularly, view resources for their research often, learn how to use resources correctly and efficiently, experiment with resources available within the disciplines, open and examine databases, become familiar with reference desk materials, find publications with abstracts of articles and books on one's topic, use papers' references to locate the most utile journals and important authors, identify keywords for refining and narrowing database searches, and peruse library catalogues online for available sources—all while taking notes.

As one searches the available literature, one will gradually develop an overview of the body of literature for his or her subject. This signals the time to prepare for writing the literature review. The researcher should assemble his or her notes along with copies of all the journal articles and all the books acquired. Then one should again write the research question at the top of a page and list below it all of the author names and keywords discovered while searching. It is also helpful to observe whether any groups or pairs of these stand out. These activities are parts of structuring one's literature review—the first step for writing a thesis, dissertation, or research paper. Writers should rewrite as necessary rather than expecting to make only one draft. However, stopping to edit along the way can distract from the momentum of the first draft. It may be better to skip to a later portion of the paper and revisit the problem section at another time.

Body and Conclusion in Literature Review

The first step of a literature review paper is to create a rough draft. The next step is to edit: rewrite for clarity, eliminate unnecessary verbiage, and change terminology that could confuse readers. After editing, a writer should ask others to read and give feedback. Additionally, the writer should read the paper aloud to hear how it sounds, editing as needed. Throughout a literature review, the writer should not only summarize and comment on each source reviewed, but should also relate these findings to the original research question. The writer should explicitly state in the conclusion how the research question and pertinent literature interaction is developed throughout the body, reflecting on insights gained through the process.

Primary and Secondary Sources

In literature review, one may examine both primary and secondary sources. Primary sources contain original information, like reports other researchers have made of their findings and other first-hand accounts written by experimenters or witnesses of discoveries or events. They may be found in academic books, journals and other periodicals, and authoritative databases. Secondary sources refer to information originally given by other people or found in other places. They may be cited, quoted, or described in books, magazines, newspapers, films, audio and video materials, databases, and websites. Accounts of research and its results are always informed and directed by reviews of the pertinent literature. These depict the present research as a cumulative process integral to the scientific method. Literature reviews also test the research question in relation to the existing knowledge about the topic.

Editing and Revising

After composing a rough draft of a research paper, the writer should **edit** it. The purpose of the paper is to communicate the answer to one's research question in an efficient and effective manner. This should be as **concise** and **clear** as possible, and the style should also be consistent. Editing is often easier to do after writing the first draft than during it, as distance allows writers to be more objective. If the paper includes an abstract and an introduction, the writer should compose these after writing the rest, when s/he will have a better grasp of the theme and arguments. Not all readers understand technical terminology or long words, so writers should use these sparingly. Finally, writers should keep a writing and style guide available to answer questions as they edit.

Review Video: Revising and Editing
Visit mometrix.com/academy and enter code: 674181

Citing Sources

Formal research writers must **cite** all sources used—books, articles, interviews, conversations, and anything else that contributed to the research. One reason is to **avoid plagiarism** and give others credit for their ideas. Another reason is to help readers find more information about the subject for further reading and research. Additionally, citing sources helps to make a paper academically authoritative. To prepare, research writers should keep a running list of sources consulted, in an electronic file or on file cards. For every source used, the writer needs specific information. For books, a writer needs to record the author and/or editor name, title, publication date, city, and publisher name. For articles, one needs the author name, title, journal (or magazine or newspaper) name, volume and issue number, publication date, and page numbers. For electronic resources, a writer will need the article information plus the URL, database name, name of the database's publisher, and the date of access.

Three common reference styles are **MLA** (Modern Language Association), **APA** (American Psychological Association), and **Turabian** (by expert author Kate Turabian). Each style formats citation information differently. Professors and instructors often specify that students use one of these. Generally, APA style is used in psychology and sociology papers, and MLA style is used in English literature papers and similar scholarly projects.

To refer to authoritative sources for citing more complicated or specialized resources, such as legislative publications, audiovisual resources, or manuscripts, see http://library.csudh.edu/cyberlib/research.htm, the section on Research and Writing Resources from the library website of California State University Dominguez Hills (CSUDH). The APA Manual is available in print: *Publication Manual of the American Psychological Association,* 6th ed., July 2009, and electronically in a Kindle edition. (The sixth is the latest edition as of February 2014.) APA has also adapted from this edition the *APA Style Guide to Electronic References,* and a pocket guide, *Concise Rules of APA Style.* Garner and Smith's *The Complete Guide to Citing Government Information Resources: A Manual for Writers and Librarians,* June 1993 (revised edition) is available in paperback on Amazon.com. *MLA Handbook for Writers of Research Papers* (7th edition, 2009) is available at MLA Bookstore's website. Turabian's *A Manual for Writers of Research Papers, Theses, and Dissertations* (8th edition, revised, 2013) is available from the University of Chicago Press website.

Review Video: Citing Sources (MLA, Chicago, APA)
Visit mometrix.com/academy and enter code: 993637

Integrating References and Quotations

In research papers, one can include studies whose conclusions agree with one's position (Reed 284; Becker and Fagen 93), as well as studies that disagree (Limbaugh 442, Beck 69) by including parenthetical citations as demonstrated in this sentence. Quotations should be selective: writers should compose an original sentence and incorporate only a few words from a research source. If students cannot use more original words than quotation, they are likely padding their compositions.

When quoting sources, writers should work quotations and references seamlessly into their sentences instead of interrupting the flow of their own argument to summarize a source. Summarizing others' content is often a ploy to bolster word counts. Writing that analyzes the content, evaluates it, and synthesizes material from various sources demonstrates critical thinking skills and is thus more valuable.

Incorporating Outside Sources

Writers do better to include short quotations rather than long. For example, six to eight long passages quoted in a 10-page paper are excessive. It is also better to avoid wording like "This quotation shows," "As you can see from this quotation," or "It talks about." These are amateurish, feeble efforts to interact with other authors' ideas. Also, writing about sources and quotations wastes words that should be used to develop one's own ideas. Quotations should be used to stimulate discussion rather than taking its place. Ending a paragraph, section, or paper with a quotation is not incorrect per se, but using it to prove a point, without anything more in one's own words regarding the point or subject, is avoiding thinking critically about the topic and considering multiple alternatives. It can also be a tactic to dissuade readers from challenging one's propositions. Writers should include references and quotations that disagree as well as agree with their thesis statements. Presenting evidence on both sides of an issue makes it easier for reasonably skeptical readers to agree with a writer's viewpoint.

Communication Processes

Relationship Between Perception and Communication

Perception and communication are inextricably linked. Our ability to understand both verbal and nonverbal communication depends on our ability to accurately interpret the information we take in from the world. In a large part, our powers of perception are based on our experiences in the world. Over time, we develop patterns of perception and observation that structure and inform our interpretation and evaluation of what is communicated to us. There is no way to avoid this process of pattern formation and, indeed, we should be thankful that our brains are capable of assimilating the massive amounts of stimuli we are bombarded by every day. At the same time, it is important to take account of our own perceptual filters so we are clearly aware of where our prejudices lie.

Relationship Between Perception and Meaning

The ability to accurately perceive is closely related to the ability to derive accurate meaning from any communication. The meanings we ascribe to the communications of others are based on our perceptions. This means in part that how we interpret what anything means is based on our perception of verbal and nonverbal communication cues. Our impression of what another person is saying comes not only from their words but from their tone of voice and body language as well. Face-to-face conversation is perhaps the most effective form of communication because it provides both parties with the most information about one another, and thus a better opportunity to correctly assess what is being conveyed. Generally, the more information one provides in any communication, the more accurate the reception of the message will be.

Low Meaning is Encoded

When one person speaks to another, he or she is "encoding" the verbal message with supplemental nonverbal forms of communication. The precise "code" the speaker uses is the particular set of words, with their agreed-upon meaning, as well as syntax and grammar. To the degree that the speaker has a command of vocabulary and a strong sense of meaning, he or she will be able to construct a subtle and effective code. The process of encoding meaning is also influenced by individual bias, desire, and perception. People encode meaning differently based on the personal "agenda" they bring to any conversation. Two people speaking to one another should be able to increase the complexity and accuracy of their message encoding as the conversation progresses because they will be acquiring more and better information about one another's intentions, knowledge, and character.

Low Meaning is Interpreted

When we listen to another person speak in conversation, we are attempting to decode their meaning through the filter of our own prejudices and perceptions. Speech communication theorists assert that listeners tend to emphasize the components of a message that are associated with their own pre-existing knowledge or interests. In particular, we all tend to emphasize the importance of those aspects of a message that directly pertain to us. Starting out, we are more likely to make mistakes in the interpretation of what a speaker is saying. As we acquire more information and become more familiar with the other person's speaking style, however, we tend to make beneficial adjustments to our interpretation. The more time we spend with another person, the better able we are to correctly interpret the meanings of their communications.

Communication Appropriate to Cooperating on a Task

For people to cooperate effectively on a task, they all need good communication skills. This is especially true in the adult professional world. Without effective communication among those involved, success will be more difficult to achieve, but many people do not learn to work effectively with others until late childhood. For the most part, any job-related task is most easily accomplished when all parties know enough about the task-related tools, ideas, and skills to communicate effectively among themselves. In some cases, two individuals working together on a task may have unequal power, such as in the case of an employer and employee collaborating on a work-related project. Such unequal distribution of power also has a strong effect on communication.

Defensiveness as an Impediment to Communication

Defensiveness is a quality that can obstruct effective communication. When one of the parties in a conversation feels threatened, he or she is likely to become defensive and protective of his or her own ego. Such a person is likely to become preoccupied with his or her own interests and fail to seriously consider the content of the other person's message. Depending on past experience and temperament, individuals have varying degrees of natural defensiveness. Unfortunately, those with greater defenses may fail to obtain new information, thus making personal progress more difficult. This in turn can prevent them from hearing valuable future criticism. As this cycle continues, defensiveness can become more deeply entrenched: stung by criticism, defensive people adopt a behavior style that is likely to lead to more criticism. Defensiveness must be challenged indirectly, as any direct challenges are likely to increase the self-protective instinct. The need to tailor one's words so as not to incite a defensive reaction in the listener takes more effort, reducing the chances of effective give-and-take.

Ulterior Motives as an Impediment to Communication

The phrase "ulterior motives" refers to intentions that are known only to one party but kept secret from the other. When one of the parties in a conversation has ulterior motives, it will be almost impossible for effective communication to take place. To a certain degree, everyone has ulterior motives in conversation, even when discussing the most banal and impersonal subjects. Each participant in the conversation essentially has his or her own personal interests at heart. However, the less forthright one is about his or her intentions in a conversation, the less likely he or she is to achieve solid understanding with the other person. Someone with a "hidden agenda" is likely to speak in a way that refers to these underlying intentions rather than to the more surface level intentions. When this is the case, the gap between stated and real intentions can lead to evasiveness and abstraction.

Importance of Feedback During Interpersonal Communication

Basically, feedback is the response that a communication message elicits from the receiver. For instance, if you are talking to a friend and that friend nods her head as you speak, she is giving you feedback that either of you understand to mean, "I agree with what you are saying", or "I understand." An entirely different message would be communicated if she started vigorously shaking her head from side to side. The amount and quality of the feedback in a conversation has a tremendous effect on the quality of the communication. As a conversation progresses, feedback allows each interlocutor to refine his or her message. This is another reason why face-to-face conversation is the format most conducive to effective interpersonal communication. In contrast, when we talk on the phone we cannot see the other person, and therefore cannot identify nonverbal forms of feedback that would allow us to refine our message appropriately.

Importance of Privacy for Effective Interpersonal Communication

In conversation, the general goal of both parties should be to create a positive environment in which self-disclosure is encouraged. Of course, there are limits to the amount of self-disclosure that is appropriate in any social interaction. There are certain thoughts and feelings that good manners and propriety keep us from expressing, even though they may influence our participation in a conversation. This need for privacy is universal. Most people have not only a desire to maintain personal privacy but also a desire to respect the privacy of others. There are certain things about other people that we simply do not want to know. What is perceived as a healthy balance between self-disclosure and privacy varies according to the relationship. For instance, a teenager will usually insist on a greater amount of privacy from his or her parents than from his or her peers. Part of the work of interpersonal communication is establishing the boundaries of self-disclosure.

How Holding Grudges Can Affect Interpersonal Communication

In some cases, interpersonal communication can be adversely affected by the unspoken resentments held by one party against the other. Anytime important information is known by one party but not the other, communication is impaired. When such information directly relates to the relationship between the two parties, a severe impairment may result. Furthermore, when an individual sits on important information and allows it to fester in his or her psyche, it may eventually emerge in a much more toxic and extreme form. Often, when an individual seems to overreact to a minor grievance, it is because he or she is consciously or unconsciously reacting to long-held grudges. For interpersonal communication to thrive conversation must be open and honest; and any important grievances must be made plain.

Basic Components of a Communication Event

Every communication event has four components: source, message, channel, and receiver. The source is the person who is speaking. The message consists of the words and the nonverbal forms of communication by which the desired information is conveyed. The channel refers to the communication venues used to deliver the message. For instance, if you encounter a friend and say "hello" while waving, you are using the channels of words and gestures. Finally, the receiver is the person or people receiving the message. For a communication event to be complete, it must include all four of these components. If there is no receiver, for example, we cannot say that a true communication event has taken place, since no information was transferred from one person to another. Similarly, if there is no message, there is nothing to communicate, and again no communication has occurred.

Process Model of Communication

Most speech communication theorists use what is called the "process model" of communication to diagram communication events. The four important components of a process model are speaker, message, channel, and receiver. These four elements will exist in any communication event, not just in a two-person conversation. For instance, consider typing an essay on a computer. During this act, all four components of the process model are represented: the "speaker" is the person typing, the message is essay the speaker is typing, the channel is the keystrokes, and the receiver is the computer on which the essay is being typed. In a conversation, the interlocutors will alternate the roles of speaker and receiver. For the most part, though, speech communication theorists find the process model to be an easy way to organize their study of communication events.

Feedback is Treated by the Process Model of Interpersonal Communication

Communications are constantly being refined and adjusted based on feedback. The process model of communication takes this into account. Indeed, the very name of this organizational scheme indicates that communication is to be thought of as an ongoing process. The process model of communication breaks the feedback process into three components: actor, goal, and observer. The actor is the person communicating and the goal is the person or thing to which the actor is trying to communicate. During a conversation, the goal is another person or a group of people, whereas during written composition the goal could be your computer. As the actor is attempting to communicate to the goal, he or she also functions as an observer, taking in whatever feedback is offered and subsequently adjusting the communication. When you receive an error message on your computer, for instance, you are receiving feedback that will influence your choices of communication in the future. This is known as a feedback loop.

Codes Used in Interpersonal Communication

The formulations of words and gestures that we use to communicate with one another are known in speech communication as codes. These are not secret codes; on the contrary, they depend for their effectiveness on our ability to understand them and we assume that they will be understood by others. Every spoken language is a code because words are used as representations of things. The names we use to describe the objects in the world and the abstract ideas in our minds are all part of the code. Furthermore, body language and hand gestures are part of a cultural code in which all of the members agree upon meaning. There is no inherit meaning in the gesture of raising one's hand and waving it, but it has been agreed upon by our culture that this gesture means greeting and welcome. To communicate effectively, one must understand both verbal and nonverbal codes and must know how to make adjustments when the receiver has an imperfect knowledge of codes.

Influences on Communication

Denotative Meaning

Denotative meaning is the way in which a word indicates something else. The word "table," for instance, denotes a flat surface with three or more legs. A speaker must always be conscious of the denotative meaning of the words he or she uses. The denotative meaning is not decided on an individual basis. Rather, it is the product of unconscious agreements on meaning made by the members of a community. In other words, to ensure that he or she communicates effectively with the audience, the speaker must have a familiarity with the denotative meanings that will be known to the members of that audience. Effective speakers continually refer to a dictionary during speech composition in order to solidify their understanding of denotative meanings.

Connotative Meaning

Connotative meaning is any implication or a suggestion connected to a word that extends beyond the denotative meaning of the word. The connotative meaning of the word, then, is not strictly the definition of the word. Connotative meanings are often quite emotional in character. For instance, the denotative meaning of the word "whale" is a large mammal that lives in the ocean. When the same word is used in a certain way, however, its connotative meaning may refer to someone who is overweight. Speakers need to be aware of both the connotative and the denotative meanings of the words they use. Otherwise, they run the risk of confusing or even offending the audience members. A detailed dictionary will often have explanations of the various connotative meanings of common words.

Role of Definitions in Communication

To be effective, a speaker must understand the basic definitions of the words he or she is using and make sure to share these definitions with the audience. If the audience members assume different definitions than those the speaker intends, there will be no possibility of communication. Speaker should always strive for clarity and precision in their choice of words. "Clarity" here means choosing words that directly convey the speaker's intended meanings. Clear language admits no confusion about the subject matter or intent. "Precise" in this context means words that do the best jobs of denoting the exact meaning intended by the speaker. When the language of a speech is precise, the audience should not have to guess what is denoted by each word.

Abstract Terms in Communication

It is easy to discover the denotative meanings of simple nouns like table, turkey, and television. It is more difficult to determine the denotative meanings of abstract nouns; that is, nouns that describe feelings, ideas, or concepts. Some examples of abstract terms are "freedom," "jealousy," and "capitalism." For the definitions of these words, a speaker must rely on a dictionary and on his own sense of how the word is used in a given community. For the most part, speakers who wish to present themselves as objective will try to make the denotative meanings of their words precise and minimize the connotative meanings as much as possible. Not only are connotative meanings more subjective for an audience, but they tend to introduce some emotional response. In other words, they compromise the speaker's objectivity.

Effective Naming in Communication

As much as possible, an effective speaker will try to choose the right words to describe his or her subject. In some cases, there may be several names for the same thing. For instance, the same car might be referred to as a sedan, an auto, or a jalopy. These three names all carry with them different connotations. Furthermore, whereas a word like "auto" suggests a certain objectivity or seriousness on the part of the speaker, a word like "jalopy" is more appropriate for a humorous or colorful speech. To maintain the right tone, then, a speaker will need to be able to select the appropriate terms. The only way to do this consistently is to develop a keen ear for language by reading widely and listening to the ways that people talk.

An effective speaker will be able to compose descriptions that clarify and illuminate his or her subject matter. For instance, consider the difference between describing a person as a "good man" and describing him as a "heroic, courageous inspiration to his community." Obviously, the second description is more colorful and paints a more comprehensive picture of the person. Indeed, it includes the information that the described person was valued for his effect on his fellow citizens. As much as possible, a speaker wants to include descriptions that combine engaging detail and vivid language, without being so colorful as to distract from the main point of the speech. A facility for effective description can be encouraged by paying attention to the way description is handled by great authors and speakers.

Effects That Cultural Background Can Have on Connotative Meaning

Members of any particular cultural group often have special connotative meanings for words. Because connotative meanings can carry such emotional power, it is especially important for a speaker to understand the connotative meanings shared by his or her audience before delivering a speech. The best way to acquire such a sense of connotative meaning is to spend time with the members of the community. Developing a feeling for what is appropriate language for a given audience is as much a matter of intuition as the acquisition of particular definitions. When in doubt, a speaker should avoid using any language that may have unpleasant or hostile connotative meaning to his audience.

Effects of Dialect on Communication

A dialect is simply a unique way of speaking that is common to a particular segment of a community. All Americans have a dialect of one sort or another. Individuals who have spent their entire lives within a given community, however, may not be aware that their mode of speech or of understanding language is different from that of any other American. To some extent, the widespread availability of television and radio has minimized the differences among American dialects. Nevertheless, a speaker needs to be aware of the dialects spoken by the members of his or her audience. Within certain dialects, common words may have unique connotative meanings that can confuse or even pervert a speaker's message. At the same time, the effective use of local dialect is a great way to endear oneself to the audience and to establish a firm channel of communication.

Avoiding Distractions While Delivering a Speech

As much as possible, an effective speaker will minimize distractions during a speech. Distractions can include things done by the audience as well as by the speaker him- or herself. Of course, it is not possible for a speaker to control the behavior of an audience, but he or she can exercise self-control. Too many speakers challenge the patience of the audience by hemming and hawing over their words, making distracting gestures, or engaging in frequent vocal tics. For many speakers, making noises like "uh" and "er" while searching for the right word is natural and unconscious. It can be very distracting to an audience, however, so a speaker would do well to practice delivering his or her message without incorporating these filler sounds.

Speaking in a Manner Appropriate to the Topic and Setting of the Speech

Ideally, with experience a speaker develops the ability to deliver his or her message in a manner appropriate to the topic, the audience, and the setting. For instance, when speaking to a group of five or six people, it is inappropriate to use a booming voice and wild, dramatic gestures. Likewise, it takes a very sophisticated speaker to deliver an intimate, informal lecture to a group of two or three hundred. One of the best ways to develop a sense of what is appropriate for a given setting is to study effective speakers in various settings. Notice how they vary their vocal quality and nonverbal communication repertoire in different environments. To gain the attention and respect of the audience, the speaker needs to deliver his or her message in a manner that will meet their expectations.

Nonverbal Communication in Establishing the Credibility of a Speaker

Many speakers underestimate the positive effects that nonverbal communication can have on their success in delivering a message. By making assertive and forceful gestures, a speaker can create an image of credibility and confidence. Similarly, by making easy gestures, a speaker can promote an image of relaxation and expansiveness. The trick is to know which gestures are appropriate in which situations. Furthermore, an effective speaker will be able to modulate the volume and pitch of his or her voice in accordance with the requirements of the speech. A bombastic tone is not appropriate to an academic discourse, nor is a dry delivery appropriate for a political rally. A speaker needs to be aware of the expectations of the audience, and only challenge them when such a challenge is necessary.

Methods of Improving Voice and Articulation Problems

For many people, delivering an effective public speech is an uphill battle because they have never mastered the basics of vocal presentation. For instance, many people have not learned the proper manner of articulating complex sounds in English. Also, many people have not received enough exposure to effective oratory and therefore do not understand the essential rhythms of speech delivery. There are a few common ways to improve voice and articulation problems. Some articulation problems are the result of physiological issues and can only be treated by a doctor. Other issues, however, are behavioral and can be resolved with therapy and training. Increasingly, schools are staffing speech clinicians to help students resolve problems with articulation.

Procedure for Improving One's Own Public Speech

The process of improving public speech technique will vary depending on the individual's particular challenges. A few common remedies can be generally helpful however. For one thing, a person can record themselves and listen to the way they speak. Speakers are frequently unaware of their articulation problems while giving a speech, but these problems become clear upon review. With practice, speakers can train themselves to diagnose particular problems and can subsequently learn to self-correct them. Practice in producing the correct sound every day should result in almost immediate progress. After a while, the corrections will become habitual and will no longer need review or practice.

Effective Listening

Forms of Listening

Other Problems of Listening Besides the SUR Listening Style

SUR is an acronym for a listening style in which the audience is self-absorbed, unfocused, and rules-driven. Unfortunately, there are some other common obstacles to listening besides being self-absorbed, unfocused, or rules-driven. Many people simply do not pay attention or they allow their minds to wander off during a digression from the major ideas of the message. In scientific studies of listening behavior, researchers have observed that the human mind can process information much more quickly than information can be delivered in a speech. Thus, while a person is listening, his or her brain is often performing other tasks simultaneously. Obviously, these other tasks run the risk of hindering effective listening and concentration. Some research has suggested, however, that many individuals require a small amount of distraction in order to concentrate effectively. For instance, many people are able to study more intently when listening to music at the same time.

Intentional Listening

Ideally, when listening to a speech one will not simply sit back and allow the words being spoken to wash over him or her. Rather, an effective listener will engage in what is known as "intentional listening," an active state of processing, interpreting, and thinking critically about a speech. It is always good for the audience members to ask themselves what they hope to gain from a speech before it begins, as this will focus their attention and give purpose to their listening. While the speaker is addressing them, audience members should be attempting to place each successive idea into an overall framework.

Appreciative and Therapeutic Listening

Speech communication researchers have identified five basic kinds of intentional listening: appreciative, therapeutic, discriminative, comprehensive, and critical. Appreciative listening is perhaps the most passive form of listening. An appreciative listener is simply seeking to obtain as much pleasure as possible from the words being spoken. Although the intention of many speeches is to entertain the audience, an appreciative listener may not pay enough attention to the actual message being delivered by the speaker. Therapeutic listening, on the other hand, is listening with the intention of obtaining as much emotional support as possible. Many times, those listening to sermons and motivational speeches are engaged in therapeutic listening. The message of the speech empowers them and makes them feel better.

Critical Listening

Speech communication researchers have identified five basic kinds of intentional listening: appreciative, therapeutic, discriminative, comprehensive, and critical. Critical listening is the most active form of audience behavior. It entails organizing and interpreting the information contained in a speech. While a speaker is giving his or her speech, the critical listener will be evaluating the arguments or ideas the speaker is presenting, weighing the evidence provided, and thinking of possible problems with the speech. As consumers, people engage in a form of critical listening every time they hear an advertisement. During a speech, however, many people sympathize with the speaker rather than critically evaluating the speaker's message.

Discriminative Listening

Speech communication researchers have identified five basic kinds of intentional listening: appreciative, therapeutic, discriminative, comprehensive, and critical. Discriminative listening focuses on the aspects of a speaker's message that are implied rather than spoken directly. A discriminative listener is paying attention to the sound of voice, body language, and the speaker's implicit argument. To a certain extent, everyone is always practicing discriminative listening, although some people engage in this style of listening more than others do. A sophisticated listener obtains information not only from the message but from the medium in which it is delivered.

Listening for Comprehension

Speech communication researchers have identified five basic kinds of intentional listening: appreciative, therapeutic, discriminative, comprehensive, and critical. Comprehensive, or listening for comprehension, is probably the most familiar form of listening. Students in a classroom are engaged in listening for comprehension when they take notes during a lecture. Whenever people listen to an informative or persuasive speech in order to gain information about a subject, they are engaged in listening for comprehension. The validity and accuracy of other forms of listening, such as critical listening and discriminative listening, depend on listening effectively for comprehension. If an individual is unable to understand the message being presented, he or she will not be able to critique it insightfully.

IMPORTANCE OF DETACHED, INTENTIONAL LISTENING

When speech communication instructors describe the ideal listener, they often refer to "detaching" or "decentering." These terms refer to the process of considering the speaker's message on its own terms rather than in the context of the listener's experience and emotions. In essence, this simply means giving a speaker a fair hearing before applying critical thinking to his or her message. Too often, audience members prejudge a message based on their past experience or existing opinions. This not only prevents such listeners from acquiring a better understanding, but it significantly handicaps their ability to listen for comprehension. Even when a speech is being delivered on a subject with which a member of the audience is quite familiar, he or she should try to keep an open mind in order to gain as much as possible from the speech.

PURPOSES OF AN AUDIENCE MEMBER MAY CHANGE DURING A SPEECH

When speech communication instructors refer to the five kinds of listening (appreciative, therapeutic, discriminative, comprehensive, and critical), they do not mean to suggest that these forms of listening exist independent of one another at all times. On the contrary, the members of an audience may be engaged in several different kinds of listening at the same time. Furthermore, it is quite common for members of an audience to adjust their listening style during the course of a speech. For instance, whereas at the beginning of a speech an audience member may be strictly listening for comprehension, as the speech goes on he or she may begin to listen more critically. Similarly, an audience member may at first pay attention strictly to the speaker's explicit message, but later may become more interested in the implications of the speech and may therefore engage more in discriminative listening.

RRA TECHNIQUE FOR ACTIVE LISTENING

When speech communication instructors describe active listening, they sometimes refer to the RRA (review, relate, anticipate) technique. This technique breaks the process of active listening down into three easy steps. To begin with, an active listener is constantly reviewing what has been said and placing new information into the evolving model of the message. As the listener considers the speaker's argument or idea, he or she relates it to his or her foundational knowledge. In other words, the audience member tries to compare and contrast the speaker's message with his or her own knowledge of the subject. Finally, an active listener tries to anticipate the rest of the speaker's message. Not only is this a good way to stay engaged with a speech, it provides an excellent measure of attention. When a listener is able to confidently predict the direction of a speech, he or she can be certain that his or her understanding of what has been said so far is sound.

HOW AN AUDIENCE MEMBER SHOULD CONSIDER THE CONTENT OF A SPEECH

When considering the content of a speech, audience members should pay special attention to three basic areas: main ideas, organization, and supporting evidence. The main ideas of the speech are the fundamental arguments or concepts the speaker is trying to convey. If the speech is effective, the main ideas will be obvious. Audience members should be paying the most attention to the articulation and elaboration of these main ideas. The way in which the main ideas are expressed and supported is referred to as the organization of the speech. For a speech to be effective, the speaker needs to organize his or her ideas clearly and avoid long digressions that obscure the main points of the speech. Finally, the audience member must consider what supporting materials the speaker is using to provide evidence for his or her ideas or arguments and must determine whether these supporting materials are appropriate and credible.

How a Listener Should Assess the Situation in Which a Speech is Given

To get the most out of a speech, a listener needs to consider all of the various factors that contribute to the speaker's message. One of the factors that does not receive a great deal of attention is the situation in which the speech is delivered. Many times, the physical and interpersonal setting in which a speech is delivered has a great deal of influence on the message. For instance, an audience member might consider whether the speaker has been required to make his or her address more or less formal for the occasion. The audience member also might consider whether the occasion on which the speech is being delivered has influenced the quality of the speaker's message. Finally, the audience member should consider whether the physical environment in which the speech is delivered has been more or less conducive to understanding and appreciating the speaker's message.

How a Listener Should Assess the Characteristics of the Speaker

As part of the overall critique of a speech, an audience member should consider the personal characteristics of the speaker. For instance, the audience member might consider what he or she knew about the speaker before the speech and then determines whether this information has had any influence on his or her interpretation of the speaker's message. The audience member might also consider whether the speaker's personal presentation indicated credibility or made his or her message difficult to believe. Many times, a speaker with a good message and solid supporting materials comes across as vague and disorganized because of his or her physical appearance and vocal mannerisms. Audience members should try to distinguish between weaknesses in the speaker's message and weaknesses in the speaker's personal presentation.

How a Listener Should Analyze the Message of the Speech

When a member of an audience listens to a speech, he or she should be paying attention to three fundamental factors: ideas, organization, and support. The most important thing to consider is whether the speaker's main ideas are logical and clearly expressed. If the ideas are comprehensible, an audience member can then consider whether the speaker has expressed those ideas in a logical order or in a disorganized way. Finally, the audience member needs to consider whether the speaker has adequately supported his or her main ideas by argument or factual evidence. Does the speaker provide enough support for his or her arguments to remain credible? Is the evidence provided relevant to the main ideas of the speech?

Benefits of Taking Notes During a Speech

One of the best things an audience member can do to organize his or her thoughts about a speech is to take notes. Taking notes during a speech allows the audience member to organize the speaker's message and mark down any questions or concerns he or she may have without becoming entangled in a long, digressive thought. Taking notes during a speech is a skill that every college student has to use on a daily basis. It is important for students to begin practicing these skills early in their academic careers. Many people believe they can accurately recall a speech in great detail, but few people actually can. Taking notes helps to refresh the memory so that an individual can accurately consider the message of the speech long after hearing it.

Process of Taking Notes on a Speech

The importance of taking clear and accurate notes during a speech cannot be overstated. Most people acquire a personal note-taking style over time. This style may be highly idiosyncratic, but it usually includes a few core features. For one thing, good note-takers usually develop a style of organization, so they can look back over their notes and discern the general structure of a speech. Indentations, margins, and numbers or letters are common ways of organizing a set of notes. It is always a good idea to leave some room on the margins of one's notes, in order to fill in any weak areas later on. Remember that notes are meant to be reviewed. After all, the primary goal of note-taking is to preserve an accurate record of the speech so that it can be recalled later.

Advanced techniques in note-taking: Over many years of study, most students develop an efficient and organized way of taking notes. There are a number of common systems of organization that have proven beneficial for top students. For instance, many students use abbreviations and shorthand so they can condense a great deal of information into a relatively small space. Using symbols that substitute for common words or expressions can save time during note-taking. Another technique is color coding one's notes; that is, using a different color pen to indicate different types of notes. Some students create elaborate outline procedures to organize the main and supporting ideas in a speech or lecture. Whereas all of these methods of note organization can be effective, it falls to the individual student to experiment and decide which best promotes his or her own understanding.

Intercultural Contact as a Characteristic of Speechmaking

An effective speaker always keeps in mind the cultural characteristics of his or her audience. When a speaker is delivering a message to an audience whose culture is different from his or her own, he or she needs to be especially sensitive to the cultural mores observed by the group. For instance, excessive familiarity may be a sign of friendliness to the speaker, but it may demonstrate disrespect in the eyes of some audiences. It is a good idea to familiarize oneself with the basic manners appropriate to the intended audience. A failure to observe the customs of the group may prevent a message from being heard.

Differences Between Listening and Hearing

For most people, listening and hearing are synonyms. In the world of speech communication, however, a subtle distinction exists between the two. Hearing is simply receiving a sound in the ear. In other words, hearing is the physiological and neurological act of converting heard sounds into meaning. Listening, on the other hand, is the more active process of taking in what is heard and interpreting it. People are constantly listening to the words of those around them and using their knowledge of language and cultural values to determine the meaning of what is being said. Listening, then, is a more subjective act than hearing.

Three Listening Styles

Experts in speech communication distinguish among three listening styles: RRP, VAT, and SUR.

RRP includes reasons-oriented listeners, results-oriented listeners, and process-oriented listeners. Reason-oriented listeners are interested in hearing the logical support for a given argument. Results-oriented listeners, on the other hand, are interested in the overall intention of the idea or argument. Finally, process-oriented listeners are interested in the way a particular idea or argument was conceived. All of these types of listeners will be very interested in the specific details of a speech. To impress an RRP listener, a speaker must have his or her details in order and possess an extensive knowledge of the subject.

VAT listeners are so-called because their listening style emphasizes the visual, auditory, or tactile elements of a speech. A visual listener will focus on the aspects of the presentation that can be seen, whether it is the speaker's body language and physical presentation or any visual aids accompanying the speech. To engage an audience of visual listeners, the speaker should be sure to have sufficient visual aids on hand. On the other hand, an auditory listener will be most interested in the spoken words delivered by the speaker. Auditory listeners will not need the presence of visual aids to hold their attention during a speech. Finally, tactile listeners need some physical contact to truly appreciate what is being described. Physical demonstrations, handouts, and sample materials are all good ways to engage the attention of a tactile listener.

SUR listening style describes those who are self-absorbed, unfocused, and rules-driven. Self-absorbed listeners are preoccupied with their own concerns and have a hard time paying attention to the ideas or interests of others. Unfocused listeners are not skilled or knowledgeable enough to listen well and thus have a hard time understanding an argument or complicated idea. Rules-driven listeners tend to obsess about minor points of reason and logic instead of paying attention to the most important aspects of a speech's message. In other words, rules-driven listeners "cannot see the forest for the trees."

Importance of Deciding to Listen

Although it may sound strange, it is actually a good idea to consciously decide to listen when involved in interpersonal communication. Most people fail to listen properly because, not being intentional listeners, they allow themselves to become distracted by secondary stimuli. When a person makes a conscious decision to listen, he or she naturally ignores all the other kinds of activity going on in the background. Also, once a person gets into the habit of consciously listening to others, he or she will find that his or her listening skills improve exponentially. Many people do not realize just how satisfying interpersonal communication can be until they make a conscious decision to listen.

Maintaining Proper Attention During a Speech

It is essential to maintain attention throughout the delivery of a speech. To get the full value of a speech, a member of the audience must understand the entire structure of the speech, and this can only be done by maintaining attention throughout. If a person misses the beginning of the speech, for example, he or she will not understand what all of the speaker's subsequent arguments and evidence are supporting. On the other hand, if an audience member listens to the beginning of the speech but allows his or her attention to trail off, he or she will come away from the speech not knowing the precise reasons why the speaker's thesis statement should be believed.

Concentrating on Message Structure During a Speech

An effective listener will be able to mentally outline the structure of a speech. The basic outline of a speech will include the main argument, supporting arguments, and supporting evidence and reasoning. Only by making sense of structure can an audience member truly assess the strengths and weaknesses of the speech. For instance, an audience member should be able to tell whether the speaker has done a good job of ordering his or her points. If the speaker makes the mistake of initiating the speech with minor points and only later working in more essential arguments, the audience members should be able to identify this error and determine whether it reflects poorly on the speaker or on the argument as a whole.

Relationship Between Good Listening and the Emotions

To be a good listener, an audience member needs to keep his or her emotions in check. Of course, this is not always easy. Sometimes a speaker's fiery rhetoric or sentimentality is designed to sweep the audience into a heightened emotional state. Audience members should try as much as possible to maintain control of their critical faculties, however, in order to accurately and objectively appraise the merits of the speech. Indeed, an objective and comprehensive speech analysis includes assessing the methods by which the speaker attempts to engage the emotions of the audience. If the audience member's emotions are roused by the speaker, he or she can say that the speaker's emotional appeal has been successful. This does not necessarily assume the merit of the speaker's argument, however.

Critical Listening as It Applies to Public Speeches

Critical listening is perhaps most important in the context of public speeches, since there will be less opportunity for each audience member to clarify the speaker's remarks through questions after the conclusion of the speech. In other words, each audience member will be on his or her own in the task of deciphering and evaluating the speaker's message. For this reason, many audience members try to take brief notes and chart out the structure of a speaker's argument. Speeches delivered to large crowds often involve appeals to the emotions. A speaker can get away with histrionic gestures and exaggerated vocal mannerisms when speaking to a large crowd, whereas these same techniques might seem ridiculous to a small group.

Principles of Rhetoric

Persuasion

Persuasion is the art of changing the attitudes, beliefs, or actions of other people. It can be used for any number of purposes: to sell a product, to make a friend, to advance a cause, or simply to win an argument. To a certain degree, even primarily informative speeches contain an element of persuasion. The speaker is encouraging his or her audience to understand a given subject in the same way he or she does. To be persuasive, the speaker must have a clear idea of what he or she is trying to accomplish. Also, it is important to understand the best persuasive strategy for achieving the desired effect Persuasion can be styled as direct argument or as more indirect, even subversive, suggestion.

Relationship Between Persuasion and Likeability

Students of rhetoric have long noticed the correlation between a charismatic personality and persuasion. Basically, if a speaker is able to establish strong personal relationships with his or her audience, he or she is much more likely to be an effective persuasive communicator. The most important thing a persuasive speaker can do is to establish trust from the outset. If a speaker can convince the audience that he or she has their best interests at heart and is a competent source of information, the work of persuasion is largely done. Establishing trust and respect with the audience is as much a matter of one's credentials as one's appearance and presentation. Speakers who can demonstrate expertise and empathy are likely to find success with the audience.

Relationship Between Persuasion and Competence

To be persuasive, an individual must be perceived as competent by the audience. Competence manifests itself in a number of characteristics, such as preparedness, poise, thoughtfulness, and clarity. A competent speaker should be able to answer questions from the audience on a specific subject, or should at least be able to explain where the answers could be found. A competent speaker must have supporting evidence for his or her arguments and must make this evidence clear to the audience. A competent speaker will also be able to organize his or her message effectively, giving the audience the best opportunity to educate themselves. Finally, a competent speaker will appear unhurried and calm.

Relationship Between Personal Conviction and Persuasion

Audiences seem to have a sixth sense for insincerity. They can tell when a speaker does not really believe his or her message. For this reason, effective persuasion is greatly benefited by the speaker's deep conviction in what he or she is saying. It is often said that before a speaker can persuade anyone else, he or she needs to be persuaded. When the strength of a speaker's convictions is evident in his or her delivery, the natural empathy of the audience will assist in persuasion. Historically, a survey of the great persuasive orators (Martin Luther King Jr., Abraham Lincoln, Pericles, etc.) confirms that strong belief is a boon to persuasive rhetoric.

Relationship Between Reputation and Persuasion

Another factor that can greatly influence a speaker's power of persuasion is reputation. When a speaker has a reputation for upright behavior and responsibility to the truth, an audience is much more likely to believe his or her message. The credibility of the speaker is imperative, regardless of the topic. If the content of the speech is highly specialized, the audience will want to know that the speaker has some advanced training in the subject. When an audience arrives for a speech already knowing the positive reputation of the speaker, the work of persuasion is almost complete. For many politicians and orators, building a reputation that encourages persuasion is the work of a lifetime.

Value of Direct Familiarity with Sources in a Persuasive Speech

Having direct knowledge of sources can be extremely beneficial to a speaker's power of persuasion. For instance, imagine a motivational speaker on the subject of weight loss. If that speaker has had the experience of being overweight and then successfully losing weight and becoming healthier, the audience will be much more likely to take his or her words to heart. When a speaker can claim direct experience of the topic on which he or she speaks, the audience is unlikely to attribute the speaker's motives to personal gain or manipulation. The most effective speakers are able to present their personal experience as a model for the examination and consideration of the audience.

Relationship Between Mimicry and Persuasion

Unconscious mimicry or imitation can be one of the most powerful forces for persuasion. Human beings have a natural tendency to imitate the behavior of those they perceive to be leaders or role models. People often adopt beliefs or act in ways uncharacteristic of who they really are in order to mirror the behavior of a leader. This phenomenon is due in part to the tendency of human beings to minimize differences between one another as a means of preventing conflict. Of course, to inspire imitation on the part of the audience, a speaker must appear competent and have a good reputation. The members of an audience should be particularly skeptical of speakers who encourage them to adopt a point of view simply because others are doing so.

Being Persuaded with Following Directions

Human beings have a natural tendency to believe what designated authority figures tell them. In part, this is an inherited characteristic. Early humans, in order to survive in the wild, often had to rely on the advice and guidance of their peers. In many cases, people will follow directions from an authority figure without considering the ramifications of their actions. This phenomenon was evidenced during the Nuremberg trials after World War II, as numerous Nazi officials defended their actions as "just following orders." The educational system also encourages people to trust authority figures and follow directions. Audience members should be aware of this tendency and should guard against blindly accepting the recommendations of a speaker.

Persuaded with Accepting a Suggestion

A persuasive speaker may sometimes use a suggestion rather than a direct command to achieve his or her goal. A suggestion is simply a less forceful recommendation; it implies that the audience has the ability to decide for themselves whether or not to accept the guidance of the speaker. Suggestion is a good strategy for dealing with naturally skeptical audience members, who will resist any overt attempts to change their minds. Because it is an indirect form of persuasion, however, suggestion requires a bit more subtlety on the part of the speaker. , But because it gives the listener the impression that he or she has arrived independently at a conclusion, suggestion can be more effective than direction.

Relationship Between Persuasion and Dramatization

A persuasive speaker often employs the language and techniques of drama to capture the interest of the audience. In other words, the speaker will frame his or her arguments as part of a larger narrative. The speaker may introduce certain representative characters and may spend a short time describing the human characteristics of these people. The speaker may then introduce some conflict against which these characters must struggle. This kind of generic dramatic scenario gives the audience a sort of "hook" on which to hang its attention. Instead of being required to pay attention to dry statistics and formal arguments, the audience can become absorbed in the stories of the characters. Many speakers find this captivation to be a spur to positive persuasion.

Relationship Between Persuasion and the Motivation of the Speaker

When an audience is considering the elements of a persuasive speech, they will likely give some thought to the motivations of the speaker. For instance, when approached by a salesperson, a customer is likely to assume that the salesperson has a vested personal interest in making a sale and does not necessarily have the best interests of the consumer at heart. In other contexts, however, the motivation of the speaker may be harder to discern. In an academic speech, for instance, the audience will be aware that the speaker is attempting to promote a certain viewpoint, but they may not be able to determine exactly why the speaker supports that point of view. To the extent that the audience can discern the motivation of the speaker, they will be able to intellectually consider the merits of the speech, and not be swayed by emotion.

Resistance to Persuasion

Audiences will naturally be resistant to persuasive arguments that attempt to take them out of their normal routine. People of all ages have a tendency to fall into habitual behaviors that can be difficult and even painful to interrupt. A persuasive speaker, however, is by nature one who attempts to convert an audience to a new way of living or thinking. He or she will therefore encounter the listeners' resistance, based on their entrenched habits. Habitual behavior can be attacked in a number of ways. One is to persuade the audience that these habits are detrimental. Another is to suggest the advantages that can be gained from a new way of living or thinking. In all cases, however, the speaker should remember that most behavioral change is incremental and not the result of sudden conversion.

Unique Qualities of a Speech that Persuades the Audience to Change

One of the most common kinds of persuasive speech is one in which the speaker attempts to persuade the audience to change something. The speaker may be asking the listeners to change their behavior, their opinion on some subject, or the way in which some issue is handled in their community. These kinds of speeches usually follow a similar arc: first, the speaker describes the disastrous state of affairs at present. Second, the speaker introduces his or her proposal for remedying the situation. Third, the speaker indicates the rewards that the audience will obtain by accepting the proposal of the speaker. If the speech is effective, by its conclusion the audience should be practically intoxicated with the expansive vision of a positive future the speaker has outlined.

Unique Qualities of a Speech That Persuades the Audience to Not Change

Another kind of persuasive speech is one in which the speaker attempts to persuade the audience to not change something. Like the speech in support of change, the speech against change has three classic components. First, the speaker argues that things are fine as they are. Second, the speaker argues against any proposals for change that have been made. Third, the speaker describes the negative consequences for the audience if changes are made. As with the speech in support of change, the speech against change begins by setting the general scene and only gradually works its way around to addressing the individual concerns of the audience members. In this way, the last impression the audience receives is that of the effects of change or stasis on their own lives.

Rhetorical Criticism

When speech communication theorists describe the process of breaking down and considering communication events, they often used the phrase "rhetorical criticism." This simply means the critical analysis of rhetoric, or spoken words. Rhetoric often refers specifically to important messages delivered to a large group of people, as for instance in a political speech. The purpose of rhetorical criticism is to improve understanding of the strategies used by speakers. When speakers develop a greater understanding of rhetorical strategy, they can refine and improve their messages, and the audience can develop a healthy degree of skepticism. In other words, rhetorical criticism can help us to become better producers and consumers of communication.

Criticism Can Be Used to Advance a Cause

Individuals frequently use rhetorical criticism to promote a particular cause they are interested in. In a democracy, making change depends on rallying the support of the public, and this in turn depends on crafting an effective message. When a group of people wants to promote a particular social or political issue, they need to develop a communication strategy that will positively influence the opinion of the general public. Advocacy groups use mailings, television ads, print ads, and speeches to deliver their message to the general public. Individuals can advocate for a cause through letters to the editor, informal speeches, and just by talking with friends. For all of these channels, a careful study of rhetorical strategy will be advantageous.

Criticism Can Solve Problems in Society

Many people use rhetorical criticism as a means to solving problems. In particular, rhetorical criticism can be applied to the problems of the society. This is especially true in a democracy, where public debate generates most of the changes in laws and social conditions. To the degree that individuals with solutions can effectively communicate their message to the general public, they will be able to persuade citizens to give their votes and support to these solutions. Without effective communication, even the most logical solutions may not achieve the critical mass of public support required to be enacted. In a similar way, politicians are constantly self-critiquing and refining their communication techniques to increase their political capital.

Criticism Can Lead to Greater Knowledge

Rhetorical criticism is able to improve our general understanding of the ways human beings communicate with one another. Most universities have several professors whose job it is to theorize and teach rhetorical criticism. The academic study of rhetoric focuses on the ways that human speech drives social change, unifies groups of people, explains societal problems, and motivates social change. In particular, the study of rhetorical criticism focuses on the way in which human speech develops and maintains individual and collective identity. Finally, rhetorical criticism takes a close look at persuasion, specifically the way in which language can motivate action in the real world.

Public Speaking

PUBLIC SPEAKING

Speech communication instructors often refer to public speaking as a "transaction," or a way of indicating the important active roles of both the speaker and audience. Too often, people consider speech-giving as a process in which one person actively provides information while another group of people passively receives information. Instead, the ideal public speaking relationship is one in which the speaker presents a message and the audience presents feedback. Even when the audience is not given an opportunity to speak, they provide feedback in the form of attention or inattention. By referring to public speaking as a transaction, instructors emphasize the roles and responsibilities of both speaker and audience. In general, speech communication instructors would define a transaction as any communication in which information passes from speaker to listener and vice versa.

PURPOSE OF STUDYING PUBLIC SPEAKING

There are a number of reasons for studying public speaking, but the most commonly cited are social, intellectual, and consumer motives. People need to learn to speak in public in order to function in society and to manage relationships, administrate social events, and minimize conflict. Intellectually, a study of public speaking gives insight into human thought, ethics, and persuasion. Public speeches can generate emotions and ideas in listeners as well as influence their existing thoughts and feelings. It is also important to study public speaking not only to improve one's own speaking skills, but to improve one's ability to analyze and interpret the speeches of others. Students need to be able to understand the forum of public expression, the rhetorical vocabulary, and the various methods of thinking critically about speech.

BASIC METHODS FOR STUDYING PUBLIC SPEAKING

An effective speech communication teacher will incorporate different pedagogical modalities into his or her instruction so that students receive exposure to a wide range of different methods. Students should practice giving different kinds of speeches in both formal and informal settings. Some of the different types of speeches include technical lectures, extemporaneous speeches, and entertaining monologues. Students should get some practice interpreting and analyzing different kinds of public speech, such as advertisements, political speeches, public service announcements, editorials, or other forms. It is also valuable for students to become familiar with acclaimed historical speeches.

GOALS OF PUBLIC SPEAKING

For most people, the obvious goals of public speaking are political victories and support for social movements. Both are common motives of public speech, but they are not the only recognized intention of public communication. Public speech is often used to define an individual or a community. For instance, people may use speeches to describe particular attributes of themselves or of the group to which they belong. People also use speeches simply to disseminate information. Speeches can be used to inspire other people to action. Famous addresses like the "I Have a Dream" speech of Martin Luther King, Jr. exemplify this kind of speech. Finally, public speaking can be used to introduce arguments and to debate controversial questions in a community. The presidential debates before the general election are a good example of this.

Speeches

Purpose of an Informative Speech

When one is delivering an informative speech, his or her primary goal is to instruct the audience on a particular subject. If the speech is effective, the audience members will leave with more knowledge and understanding. College lectures are a great example of an informative speech. Although informative speeches may be entertaining, the humor or "color" of the speech should not distract from the overall intention, which is to disseminate information. Informative speeches often contain specific statistical data and an organized set of arguments and supporting evidence. Many informative speeches contain mention of counter-arguments, including rebuttals.

Impromptu Speech

An impromptu speech is one delivered "off-the-cuff"; that is, one delivered with a minimum amount of preparation and in an informal style. Not everyone is capable of delivering an effective impromptu speech. Most people can give a successful impromptu speech only if the topic is one on which they have discoursed before or if they are extremely familiar with their topic. Of course, we all make impromptu speeches as a matter of course in our daily lives. Every time you are asked to give your opinion on a subject or to explain an idea, you are in effect making an impromptu speech. By studying speech communication, however, people can learn the elements of effective impromptu speeches and improve their ability to deliver them.

Extemporaneous Speech

An extemporaneous speech combines elements of preparation and improvisation. When one is delivering an extemporaneous speech, he or she is drawing on prepared research but not reading directly from a sheet of paper nor reciting the speech from memory. An extemporaneous speech is more conversational and informal than a written speech and is therefore more appropriate for casual gatherings. The colloquial and informal nature of an extemporaneous speech can be extremely helpful in cultivating a good rapport between speaker and audience. To deliver an effective extemporaneous speech, however, the speaker must be extremely familiar with his or her source material.

Eulogy

A eulogy is a speech that praises a particular individual and highlights his or her best qualities. Eulogies are often given at funerals as the speaker remembers the deceased in a positive light. Eulogies are not the appropriate form for criticism or objective analysis of a person's life. On the other hand, a eulogy may fail if the audience finds it so excessively laudatory that it is not believable. In some cases, a eulogy of sorts may be given in praise of a particular event, community, or culture. Typically, a eulogy is delivered to an audience that is already disposed to think favorably of the subject. The speaker is typically someone who has extensive personal experience with the subject of the eulogy.

Introductory Speech

It is common for a speech of introduction to precede a keynote speech, a presentation, or a public performance of some kind. For instance, a symphony director will often give a brief speech of introduction before a concert. The best introductory speeches do not simply list the achievements or characteristics of the person or event that is to follow. Rather, they engage the interest of the audience and whet their appetite for what is to come. A good speech of introduction should not include any criticism of what is to follow. It is always a good rule of thumb for the introductory speaker to confer with those who are to follow so that his or her message can be as appropriate as possible.

Welcoming Speech

A welcoming speech is often given at the beginning of a convention, meeting, or special event of some kind. Typically, the welcome will be delivered by a representative of the group or organization putting on the event. For instance, the chairman of a professional organization administering a business convention might deliver a speech of welcome to convention attendees. Welcoming speeches are typically light on substance and primarily provide an overview of the events to follow. Also, a welcoming speech typically includes a message of thanks to the organizers and administrators of the event. The speaker often indicates his or her personal goals for the event and may tell the audience how to make their questions and comments known to the event administrators.

Memorizing and Reading a Speech

When delivering a speech, the speaker may need to decide whether to memorize or read the text. There are advantages to each approach. When a speech is memorized, the speaker can make eye contact with the audience and use his or her hands to make illustrative gestures. Memorized speeches run the risk of sounding overly rehearsed, however, and the speaker may falter if he or she loses track of the speech. Some speakers prefer to read their speeches, often because they prefer to have a copy of the speech for reference. If the speaker plans to read his or her speech, he or she should become extremely familiar with the speech so it is not necessary to read every word from the paper. Regardless of whether a speech is memorized or read, the speaker should practice delivery to increase fluency.

Purpose of a Persuasive Speech

Persuasive speeches are designed to change the minds of the audience or motivate the audience to action. The precise goals of a persuasive speech are dependent on the particular cause promoted by the speaker. Moreover, the methods employed in a persuasive speech will depend on the subject matter and the speaker's rhetorical style. Some speakers employ a dry, data-driven style when making a persuasive speech. They hope to overwhelm their audience with the strength and breadth of information. Other speakers seek to beguile their audience by amusing and entertaining them. This kind of speech is appropriate for general audiences and non-technical subjects. When a persuasive speech is being delivered to an audience of experts, or is centered on a complex issue, it must include cogent reasoning and supportive data.

Purpose of an Entertaining Speech

The only goal of some speeches is to entertain and amuse the audience. Standup comedy is a type of entertaining speech. Many speeches that also contain information or persuasive content are primarily entertaining. The keynote speakers at conferences and conventions often cloak their arguments in witty anecdotes and jokes. Obviously, serious subjects are not appropriate content for entertaining speeches. However, many speakers will introduce some elements of an entertaining speech to first capture the attention of the audience and then persuade them to engage seriously with the more weighty elements of the speech.

Importance of Having Specific Purposes for a Speech

The first step in preparing a speech is knowing the specific purpose of that speech. This enables the speaker to focus on what is important and to research efficiently for relevant material. Knowing the specific purpose of the speech allows the speaker to emphasize the most important points within the speech. The specific purpose of a speech might be informing the audience on a particular point, changing a few minds on a particular subject, raising some money, or simply entertaining the audience. It is a good idea to make the specific purpose of the speech explicit in the speech. Although you do not want to beat your audience over the head with your intentions, there should be no question as to what the speech is meant to accomplish. In general, the specific purpose of a speech is defined in terms of the desired reaction from the audience.

ELEMENTS OF A PRESENTATION

Over the last few years, the presentation has emerged as the most common speech form in the United States. Members of the business community frequently give presentations, but this form is also common to academic lectures, community discussions, and religious gatherings. One of the defining characteristics of a presentation is that it contains other media besides simply a speaker. It is common for a speaker to include slide shows, photographs, brochures and handouts, short videos, audio samples, in a presentation. Because presentations are often designed to be given over and over again to different audiences, they may be complex, detailed, and highly coordinated.

BASIC PRESENTATION AID

One of the defining characteristics of a presentation is the use of presentation aids. Speakers often include supplementary audio or visual materials that elaborate or reinforce their presentation points. Currently, the most popular presentation aid is slide shows, a software program that allows speakers to assemble a collection of slides to accompany their speech. Speakers also frequently include video samples in their presentations. In business, tables and charts are frequently used to illustrate the points of a presentation. In the classroom, a teacher might use handouts or overhead projector transparencies as presentation aids. Basically, any media used by the speaker to supplement his or her spoken message is considered a presentation aid.

INCREASING IMPORTANCE OF THE PRESENTATION IN THE UNITED STATES

Most speech communication experts believe that presentations will increasingly become the most popular form of public communication. In large part, this is because the citizenry of the United States has been raised on television and radio commercials. That is, they are well used to multimedia presentations. For many people, a simple speech is boring. Presentation aids such as audio and video are often necessary to hold the interest of modern-day audiences. In the future, the most successful persuasive speakers will undoubtedly be those who can apply the traditional elements of direction and suggestion to a presentation containing enough multimedia to engage the interest of the audience.

PREMISE OF AUDIENCE ANALYSIS

In the study of speech communication, audience analysis is simply the practice of examining the characteristics and background of the audience in order to tailor a speech appropriately. For instance, one would want to know the general age, socioeconomic status, culture, and gender of an audience while preparing a speech. The type of speech appropriate to a group of elementary schoolgirls will be quite different from that appropriate to a group of older men, even if both speeches are on the same subject. The prejudices and pre-existing opinions of these two groups will be extremely different and thus, to be effective, a speaker must tailor and deliver his or her message to each group in very different ways.

PRIMARY FACTORS OF AUDIENCE ANALYSIS

When a seasoned public speaker conducts an audience analysis, he or she focuses on a few specific characteristics of the audience. For one thing, the speaker wants to know the audience's background as it relates to him or her and his or her subject matter. Although much of audience analysis consists of determining the approximate ages and socioeconomic backgrounds of the audience, this is primarily because such information enables the speaker to estimate the audience's opinions and degree of familiarity with the subject matter and speaker. A speaker who is well-liked by the audience can employ a different rhetorical strategy than one with whom most of the audience disagrees.

Importance of Remembering the Audience's Capacity to Act

When developing a speech, one should always remember the characteristics and capabilities of the audience. This is especially important when producing a persuasive speech. It does not make sense to encourage the audience to take an action they are not capable of taking. For instance, a politician would be foolish to make an impassioned plea for votes to a bunch of elementary school students, all of whom are years away from voter eligibility. When developing a persuasive speech, then, it is essential to remember the capacity of the audience to act.

Audience Attitude

It is important for a speaker to gauge the attitude of the audience before delivering his or her speech. Attitude, because it is more subtle than age, ethnicity, or belief system, can only be determined through direct observation. Thus, if a speaker is able to observe the audience before delivering the speech, he or she can benefit greatly. Observing the audience beforehand can provide clues to what kind of general mood the audience is in, whether good or bad. If the audience is in a hostile mood, the speaker may want to avoid trying to joke with them. An audience that seems jovial and engaged, on the other hand, should not be alienated with strident rhetoric or harsh words. The job of the speaker is to establish and maintain a good rapport with the audience.

Beliefs

To accurately assess what an audience might be thinking, one must understand that audience's core beliefs. Strictly defined, beliefs are the facts, ideas, and opinions that the audience holds to be true. Objectively, some of these beliefs may actually be untrue. However, to deliver an effective message, a speaker must take into account the sum total of the audience's beliefs. If the purpose of the speech is to adjust the beliefs of the audience, the speaker must appeal to either the reasoning skills or the emotions of his or her listeners.

Facts and Opinions

When considering the convictions of an audience, it is good to distinguish between facts and opinions. Facts are those convictions that can be proven in an objective sense. Scientific assertions, for instance, are considered facts. Opinions, on the other hand, cannot necessarily be supported by hard data. People often hold opinions for rather arbitrary individual reasons, such as those based on personal experience. The fact that communities hold collective opinions must also be considered when making a speech. In general, it is easier for a speaker to adjust beliefs or convictions based on opinion than those based on fact.

Fixed and Variable Beliefs

When describing the beliefs of an audience, speech communication instructors often distinguish between fixed and variable beliefs. The primary difference between the two is that fixed beliefs are harder to change. Typically, fixed beliefs have been held throughout an individual's life and most likely reinforced by his or her experience. Variable beliefs, on the other hand, may have been recently acquired and therefore may be less established in the individual's mind. A speaker is more likely to change variable beliefs and should therefore focus his or her attention on these. Variable beliefs are especially vulnerable to change when they are based on opinion rather than fact.

Fundamentals of Preparing a Speech

To successfully prepare a speech it is best to follow a basic set of established steps. By following these steps, the speaker (or speechwriter) can more efficiently develop an organized and effective presentation. The first step in preparing a speech is to select a subject, if the topic has not been predetermined. Next, the speaker should articulate to himself or herself the key ideas and arguments to be included in the speech. As he or she begin to formulate these ideas and arguments, it is important to take into account the characteristics of the intended audience. At this point, the speaker should begin gathering materials for the speech, whether through research or brainstorming. The next step is to outline the speech, and finally, write a draft of the speech. It is always a good idea to practice delivering the speech and to make revisions or adjustments where necessary.

Select a Subject for a Speech

Perhaps the most important component of an effective speech is an appropriate and interesting subject. When selecting a subject for a speech, one should look for a topic that is engaging to a general audience. While it is important for the speaker to have some familiarity with the subject, it is not necessarily a good idea to speak about a subject on which he or she is an expert. Too often, an expert delivering a speech to a general audience dwells too much in details and specificities, which has a tendency to bore the audience. It is a good idea for the speaker to have a passing familiarity with the subject, so that he or she will be able to find good research materials and judge what will be interesting to a general audience. However, the speaker should also make sure to emphasize the aspects of the subject that are relevant to the lives of the audience members.

Creativity Can Be Used to Select a Speech Topic

Sometimes it can be difficult to come up with a topic for a speech. All the "good topics" may seem to have already been covered, or there may be no one single subject on which a potential speaker has enough information to be effective. Effective speakers develop creative ways to come up with new speech topics. Being creative, however, does not mean sitting back and waiting for the muse of speech topics to visit. Creative speakers work proactively to develop new topics. They list their areas of interest and are constantly considering everything they see and read in terms of how it could be developed into a speech. Most creative speakers discard more ideas for speeches than they ever use.

Creative Analysis of a Speech Topic

After a speaker has decided upon a topic for a speech, the next move is to conduct a creative analysis of that topic—simply a detailed exploration of the topic. To begin with, the speaker assembles as much information as he or she can within the amount of time available. This may include interviews, books, and old periodicals. Experienced speakers will have a good working knowledge of the public or school library and will be able to acquire diverse basic materials in a short period of time. After all this information has been assembled, the speaker will sort through it, looking perhaps for an entry point for his exploration. An interesting narrative, a point of local interest, or a previously overlooked angle on the subject may all be ways for the speaker to engage the interest of the audience on a given subject.

Preparation Phase of a Speech

During the preparation phase of speech composition, a speaker will begin to organize his or her research material. Once the speaker has decided upon the basic angle and structure of the speech, he or she may need to acquire more research materials for elaboration and support. Of course, it may take the speaker a while to find the appropriate thrust of the speech. Speakers should not be discouraged by numerous blind alleys or false starts during the preparation phase. Even when it seems that progress is not being made, the speaker should remember that each false start eliminates a possible point of entry bringing the ultimate goal closer.

Incubation Phase of Creative Speech Analysis

During the incubation phase of creative speech analysis, the speaker actually does not engage in any direct work on the speech. Instead, the speaker allows his or her subconscious to mull over the content of the speech. Even though it seems like no work is being done during this period, the incubation phase is actually very important, as it is during this period that the most creative thinking on the subject occurs. Also, the incubation phase gives the speaker a chance to freely imagine the speech, associate various ideas, and try unique combinations. Many speakers say their most unique and powerful ideas often occur to them when they are doing something totally different than speech preparation.

Illumination phase of creative speech analysis: After the incubation phase, the speaker should have a solid structure as well as a number of creative ideas for the speech. In the succeeding illumination phase, he or she will apply the ideas gained during the incubation phase to the basic outline constructed during the preparation phase. It is very common for a speaker to feel a burst of enthusiasm during the illumination phase, as he or she discovers the unique ways in which his or her original ideas will elaborate and improve upon the original structure. The illumination phase is still basically a brainstorming phase. Speakers are still experimenting with new ideas and combinations of materials.

Verification phase of creative speech analysis: The fourth and final part of the creative analysis of a speech topic is the verification phase. During this phase, the speaker looks over his or her notes carefully. Occasionally, some of the ideas that seemed so brilliant during the incubation and illumination phases turn out to be inappropriate or implausible. Other times, a careful examination of the speech will uncover holes in the reasoning of the argument or reveal the necessity of adding or removing a particular part of the speech. The verification phase of creative speech analysis can be seen as a final polishing of the materials gathered and organized during the first three phases.

Necessity of Managing Creativity During the Development of a Speech

For the process of creative speech analysis to be effective, a certain amount of discipline needs to be brought to bear on the creative instinct. This is one reason why the process of creative speech analysis includes four distinct phases. By adhering to a set procedural pattern, the speaker will limit the amount of time spent in any one area and will move along toward completion at a predictable pace. Also, by following an organized analysis process, it is easier to avoid the procrastination that commonly occurs during the creative process. As much as possible, a speaker should try to work at specific times without interruption to allow the creative subconscious to do its work.

Basic Message Units in a Speech

In every speech, the content is divided into what are called basic message units. A basic message unit has two parts: the point the speaker is trying to make and the evidence or supporting material he or she has assembled. In order to be complete, a message unit needs to have both components. Otherwise, the speaker will be making points without offering any reasoning or evidence, or he will be giving factual information and argumentation without connecting the dots to make a larger point. The point stated by the speaker needs to be a complete and discrete thought. The supporting material must be pertinent to the point and sufficient to convince a reasonable person.

Value of Making a Logical Analysis of a Speech Topic

A speaker should always perform what is known as a logical analysis before presenting his or her speech. This is simply an analysis of the message units that make up the speech, as well as the connections between these message units. To be effective, the logic of any speech must progress in a systematic and discernible manner and should include ample evidence and supporting materials.

Speakers often create a brief outline for their speech, in which they sketch the basic structure of the speech's logic, leaving out the supplementary material. In any case, it is essential to make sure the logical skeleton of a speech is sturdy before focusing on other aspects.

Assess the logic of a speech topic: As the speaker reviews his prepared speech and performs a logical analysis, he needs to be constantly asking himself whether each point and piece of supporting material is essential. Everything included in the speech should be there for a clear and explicit reason or else it must be considered superfluous. The speaker must also determine whether all of the evidence clearly and directly supports the points it is intended to support. Finally, the speaker must make sure every point in the speech follows a proper order, progressing logically to the speech's climax and ultimate conclusion.

Error of Reasoning: Faulty Attribution of Causation

One of the most common errors of logic one can make in a speech is the faulty attribution of causation. This occurs when the speaker erroneously assumes that just because one thing followed another, the second thing was caused by the first. For instance, I may grab my umbrella on the way out the door before it starts raining, but if I later use my umbrella I cannot claim that bringing my umbrella caused the rain. When a speaker describes a major historical or social event and suggests such an event had only one cause, this is almost always a case of faulty attribution of causation. Major social and historical movements are simply too complex to be attributed to a single cause. At the very least, a speaker must provide detailed substantiation for any assertions of causation.

Error of reasoning: circular reasoning: A common logical error in speeches is circular reasoning. A chain of logic is described as circular when the assumptions made at the beginning of the argument depend on the conclusion of the argument being true. For instance, imagine a speaker declaring that the Tigers baseball team will certainly lose their playoff series. As evidence for this claim, the speaker declares that the Tigers always lose their playoff series. This reasoning clearly does not hold up: In order to believe the Tigers will lose their playoff series, we have to assume they always lose their playoff series, which we do not really know yet, and which depends on their performance in the upcoming playoffs series. In other words, the claims made by the speaker depend for their support on the speaker's assumptions.

Error of reasoning: contradictory argument: Occasionally, a speaker will fall victim to the logical error known as the contradictory argument. A contradictory argument is one in which the speaker introduces information that directly contradicts his main argument. For the most part, this error should be easy to avoid. After all, a speaker will be careful not to include information that undermines his main point. Speakers do, however, sometimes include inconsistent arguments in a speech and this can be highly detrimental to their purpose. Contradictory argument is especially problematic in a persuasive speech, in which the speaker is attempting to persuade the audience from their pre-existing opinions and hoping to sell them on the merits of an alternative view.

Use of Expository Supporting Material

Most speeches include expository supporting material. The word "expository" comes from the same root as "expose" and refers to information that sheds light on areas about which the audience may know little. Some of the common forms of expository information are examples, analogies, and narratives. Expository supporting material is distinguished from argumentative supporting material in that it strives to remain as objective as possible When a speaker claims to be providing objective and impartial information, he or she will be held to that standard by the audience. For this reason, it is especially important for speakers who use expository supporting material to verify their sources.

Use of Examples, Both Real and Hypothetical

Successful speakers are likely to use both real and hypothetical examples in the course of a speech. Real examples are appropriate in speeches describing a particular historical or social topic that is grounded in reality. For instance, it would not be appropriate to use a hypothetical example in an argument about the Revolutionary War since there are plenty of real examples to illustrate points regarding that conflict. In more general speeches, however, it may be necessary to use a hypothetical situation as an example. When describing the possible results of some decision, for instance, a speaker might invoke the case of some hypothetical person as a means of dramatizing his or her argument. In general, real examples are treated with more respect by an audience and should be used whenever possible.

How a good speaker uses examples: A good speaker knows that examples can be effective because they provide concrete case studies through which the audience can assess the arguments of the speech. Examples are also good for humanizing an abstract speech. For instance, an audience may have a hard time listening to a speech about water conservation, but if the speaker introduces examples of how drought can affect individual people, they will be more likely to stay engaged. A good speaker includes examples that are appropriate and interesting, but which do not distract from his or her main points. Also, examples should not dominate a speech; they should simply add interest to the body of the speaker's message.

Analogies in a Speech

An effective speaker will often elaborate and clarify his or her ideas with analogies. An analogy is simply an extended comparison between two things. For instance, a speech on economics might describe a current downturn in the economy as it relates to the Great Depression. In other words, the speaker is drawing an analogy between a current problem and a known historical event. The important thing to remember about an analogy is that the two things being compared will probably not be identical in all respects. The speaker should take care to indicate this and should not make claims that suggest the analogy is perfect. On the other hand, an effective analogy can be a useful predictive tool and can give the audience a way of engaging with the subject.

Narratives in a Speech

Speakers often incorporate narratives into their speeches as a way of engaging interest and indirectly making a point. A narrative is simply a story. Narratives can be either fiction or nonfiction. As with examples, narratives tend to have more impact on an audience when they are true. However, an artfully told fictitious narrative can also captivate an audience. Recent scientific research suggests that audience members are mentally programmed to pay attention to information when it is presented as a story. That is, the human mind is naturally receptive to a narrative. Good speakers take advantage of this tendency by delivering information in the context of a narrative.

Statistics in a Speech

Speakers often use statistics to provide numerical evidence for their assertions. Basically, a loose definition of statistics is any information that contains numbers. To be effective, statistics must be clear and accurate. Statistics can have a great deal of sway over an audience, since they carry with them the impression of objectivity and mathematical truth. That being said, audience members should keep in mind that statistics are often highly subjective. For instance, by manipulating sample size, information taken into consideration, and scope of a statistical survey, a speaker can present information to support his point no matter how incorrect it is. Audience members should always be wary of statistics and should press the speaker to provide more information on the origin and methodology behind any statistics he or she uses.

NUMBERS IN A SPEECH

There are a few different ways to use numbers in a speech. One way is to use numbers as markers of evaluation. When we say a person weighs 120 pounds, for instance, we are using numbers to evaluate their weight. In a similar way, numbers can be used as a basis for comparison. By comparing the prices of two dishwashers, for instance, we obtain an important piece of information we can use in making a consumer decision. Numbers can also be used to make illustrative points. For instance, speakers often cite various statistics in support of an argument. It is important to emphasize that, although numbers suggest impartiality, they are calculated by human beings, who are highly subjective and whose intentions should be rigorously questioned.

EYEWITNESS TESTIMONY IN A SPEECH

Many speakers incorporate eyewitness testimony into their speeches to great effect. Of course, this kind of supporting material is only appropriate for certain kinds of speeches. For instance, when delivering a speech about the Battle of the Bulge, it might be very useful to quote some soldiers who fought in the battle. On the other hand, eyewitness testimony seems less appropriate to a speech about climate change , which is so widespread that no one person could view its entire effect globally. When using eyewitness testimony, it is important to establish the credentials of the person being quoted. Also, a speaker should take care to indicate the particular vantage point of the eyewitness, so the audience can consider his or her testimony in light of that point of view.

EXPERT TESTIMONY IN A SPEECH

Whenever possible, speakers attempt to incorporate expert testimony into their speeches. Any time a speaker can quote a well-known authority who agrees with his or her point of view, he or she will be eager to do so. Most members of an audience will probably feel relatively uninformed compared to the speaker and will be ready to listen to anyone who may be considered an expert. Of course, testimony is only expert and appropriate when it comes from an expert in that particular field. For example, most people would be less inclined to take seriously the political views of an expert in basketball than they would if those views came from a respected public servant. Nevertheless, an audience should remain skeptical about persuasive arguments, even when they are made by experts. The standards of logic required of experts apply to everyone else as well.

ETHICS IN PUBLIC SPEAKING

To be effective as a public speaker, one needs to maintain a high degree of ethical rectitude. This is true not only because of the inherent virtues of ethical behavior, but also because an audience will not trust a speaker whom they believe to be unethical. To promote good ethics as a public speaker, one should always be as honest as possible. One should also try to promote the interests of the audience whenever appropriate. It is important to give members of the audience responsibility for making up their own minds, rather than attempting to browbeat them into submission with one's argument.

TITLE OF THE SPEECH

It is very important to settle on a clear and appropriate title for a speech early on in the preparation process. The title should make explicit the central idea or concept to be discussed in the speech. The title should also indicate the intention of the speech. For instance, if the intent of the speech is to inform the audience about a particular subject, the title should clearly state the name of the subject. If the intention of the speech is to persuade the audience, the title should indicate the main arguments to be made by the speech. To be effective, a title should be succinct, clear, and, if possible, engaging.

Difference Between Immediate Aim and Ultimate Aim When Making a Speech

On occasion, a speaker will have a slightly different intention in making a speech than is apparent from the speech itself. In the field of speech communication, this is known as the distinction between immediate aim and ultimate aim. An example would be a particular speech intended to be a small part of achieving a long-term goal. A prominent businessman, for example, might make a speech about ethics in public policy. Whereas on its face the speech might seem to be a simple address about local community issues, it might be also be part of the businessman's plan to develop his reputation in advance of a political campaign. The immediate aim of the speech, then, is to inform, while the ultimate aim is to advance the political ambitions of the speaker.

Location Should Dictate the Characteristics of the Speech

When preparing a speech, one should always keep in mind the occasion for which the speech is intended as this will help determine what kind of speech is appropriate. Individuals who have gathered together for a summer picnic, for instance, will not be interested in hearing a long and complicated speech. A short, humorous address would be more appropriate for this setting. A convention of professors, on the other hand, will be receptive to a more substantive speech that might also include relevant technical information. On rare occasions, a speaker may decide it is necessary to deliver a speech not entirely appropriate for the setting; this should only be done, however, when it is absolutely necessary.

Time Limits Influence the Preparation of the Speech

When preparing a speech, one must be aware of exactly how much time is available for presenting the material. The time limit will greatly influence the content of the speech. It is rarely possible, for instance, to effectively discuss a complicated subject in a short period of time. Nor will it be possible to hold an audience's interest over a long period of time without having a wealth of information and ideas. Giving an effective persuasive speech in particular requires sufficient time. This is especially true when one is trying to convert an audience's opinion on a subject with which they are unfamiliar or on which they already have firm opinions. Generally, it takes a strong argument, elaborated through a number of points, to alter an opinion already agreed upon by most members of the audience.

Elements of Setting a Speaker Should Consider When Preparing a Speech

When preparing a speech, a speaker should take into account any idiosyncrasies of the speech format or setting. For instance, in some situations a speaker will have specific guidelines and rules for his or her speech. When giving an address to the members of a particular religious or cultural group, for instance, one might need to abide by specific rules. Another thing to consider is the placement of the speech in the overall event. For instance, if other speeches are to follow, one might want to make sure there will be no overlap in speech content. Also, if the speech is to be given directly after a dinner, one should be aware that audience members will be less likely to pay close attention to the details of the speech. Finally, a good speaker will be aware in advance what the physical setting for the speech will be. That is, he or she will know beforehand such details as whether or not the speech is to be given standing or sitting and whether a podium will be available.

Research Required Preparing for a Speech

To adequately prepare for delivering a speech, one needs to assemble all pertinent information and create a complete outline. One of the reasons why it is a good idea to select a familiar topic for one's speech is that less research will be required. At the very least, one should know where to look to find the information necessary to deliver an informative and comprehensive speech. Speakers may need to consult with experts in the given subject or peruse newspapers, magazines, and books for extra information. Many local and school libraries have extensive databases for performing research, and a thorough Internet search can often provide vast amounts of helpful material.

Composing a Speech Outline

Creating a detailed, comprehensive outline is the first step before actually writing the first draft of a speech. After assembling all the necessary material and information for the speech, the speaker can then begin organizing the main points of the speech and the arguments and evidence supporting his or her ideas and claims. It is important that all secondary ideas and claims also support the speech's main idea or claim. One should always introduce the most important claim, or thesis, at the beginning of the speech. The speaker can then spend the rest of the speech building a case for this thesis and elaborating other related points. When composing an outline, remember that the finished speech should ideally be much more colorful and engaging. An outline is not meant to entertain, but rather to clearly and succinctly indicate the organization of the speech.

Practicing Speech Delivery

Excellent speech delivery does not just happen. It is the result of extensive practice. After the speaker has outlined and drafted the speech, he or she needs to practice delivering it. Practicing a speech serves a number of purposes. For one thing, the speaker might not detect weak points in the speech until he or she actually speaks the words aloud. In addition, it is helpful to record oneself practicing the speech and then play back the tape to identify weaknesses in the delivery. It is often a good idea to practice delivering a speech in front of friends or family and then have them critique the performance. Perhaps the most important point is that practice delivering the speech allows the speaker to further familiarize him or herself with the material, thus increasing the level of comfort and fluency in delivery.

Methods for Cultivating Self-Confidence While Giving a Speech

Most people struggle with some degree of anxiety when they are required to speak in public. One of the best things a person can do to reduce speech anxiety is to present a confident image. Naturally, one should always practice delivering a speech several times beforehand. Through repetition, the speaker becomes familiar with the appropriate gestures and rhythms of the speech, which gives rise to increasing confidence in his or her ability to deliver. Another good way to build confidence is to make eye contact with the audience during speech delivery. A forthright, steady gaze from the speaker connotes a feeling of confidence. Finally, confidence can be communicated through posture and body language. Standing up straight and emphasizing key points with hand gestures is a great way to communicate self-confidence.

Essential Points of Speech Evaluation

There are a number of things to look for when evaluating the quality of a speech. All effective speeches share a few essential characteristics, such as a good introduction—one that engages the audience and introduces the main idea or argument of the speech. The introduction also establishes the tone of the rest of the speech. The body of the speech should include clear exposition of ideas and appropriate supporting material. The conclusion of the speech should reinforce the main idea or claim and solidify audience understanding. The presentation of the speech should be appropriate to the audience and setting and should be fluent in its delivery.

Basic Elements of Speechmaking

To master the speechmaking process one should clearly understand a few basic elements. The central figure is the speaker; that is, the one delivering the speech. The speaker brings a self-conception as well as a conception, or impression, of the audience's general identity. In the study of speechmaking, the audience is sometimes referred to as the "receiver." Like the speaker, the audience members will have a self-image as well as an impression of the speaker. The setting in which the speech is delivered is known as the "situation." The speaker uses various channels of communication, including words and gestures, to communicate his or her message. The audience members will deliver their responses to the speech both verbally and through body language. This response to the speech is called feedback.

Basic elements of the message of a speech: The message of a speech is communicated not only with the words being spoken but also through the speaker's self-presentation. In other words, the quality of the speaker's voice and his or her body language contribute to the message as well. The message of the speech is generally considered to have three basic components: structure, content, and presentation. The structure of the speech is the order in which information is delivered. To be effective, a speech must have a logical and coherent structure. The content of the speech is the information it contains; even an entertaining or persuasive speech must have good content. Finally, the presentation of a speech is the style in which it is delivered to the audience. Different kinds of speeches require different presentation styles. The most important thing is to match the presentation to the intention of the speech.

Most Important Attributes of a Speaker

To be an effective speaker, one must have a clear intention, a good attitude, and extensive knowledge of the subject of the speech, as well as a degree of credibility with the audience. The speaker should fully understand the intention of the speech, even if that intention is not directly expressed in the speech. Sometimes a speaker will have a hidden motive or a long-term goal that cannot be expressed in the speech. To establish credibility, the speaker should possess a solid working knowledge of the subject of the speech. When the speaker is fluent in the subject he or she is discussing, the speech will flow more naturally and the speaker will be able to tailor his or her message to the audience's level of understanding. Referring to a speaker's "attitude" simply means his or her self-conception; that is, the image the speaker has of himself or herself. If a speaker has a positive self-image, he or she is more likely to deliver an effective speech.

Characteristics of the Speech Listener

The individual or groups of individuals who listen to a speech bring their own characteristics to bear on the quality of the speech. For one thing, listeners will always have their own intentions. That is, they will always be seeking to obtain something from the speech, whether it is information or entertainment. Listeners will also have varying degrees of skill, meaning that some groups will be better at understanding a complex message. Listeners will also bring their pre-existing attitudes toward the speaker and the speaker's subject. To deliver an effective message, a speaker needs to perform an audience analysis to determine the characteristics of his or her listeners.

Basic Kinds of Feedback

Feedback is the response of the audience to the message delivered by a speaker. Although feedback is typically thought of as verbal responses to the message, it also includes body language, attention or inattention, and participation in dialogue after the speech. To be effective, a speaker must be attuned to all these kinds of feedback. In other words, he or she must monitor the audience throughout the speech to identify signs of boredom or engagement. The feedback a speaker receives while delivering his speech is called immediate feedback. The feedback the speaker receives after delivering the speech is called delayed feedback. Delayed feedback usually takes the form of critical comments, praise, or questions. A practiced speaker will use feedback to improve subsequent speeches.

Importance of Selecting a Subject Appropriate to the Time Limits of the Speech

Many speakers handicap themselves from the start by selecting a subject that is either too expansive or too narrow for their needs. To be effective, a speech subject must be appropriate for the amount of time available for giving the speech. Obviously, a half-hour speech can go into much more detail and tackle a wider range of issues than can a five-minute speech. A very short speech should have only one main idea, whereas in a longer speech the speaker may have time to deliver several important points and give supporting information for each. Although the best way to determine the appropriate subject for the time limit is to gain experience as a public speaker, beginning speakers can nevertheless help themselves by considering the parameters of a speech as they begin to consider possible subjects.

Tailoring the Subject of a Speech So That It Is Appropriate to the Audience

When deciding on the subject of the speech, the speaker must take into account the characteristics and ability level of the audience. The speaker should be aware of the audience's expectations. That is, whether they expect to be informed, entertained, or persuaded. Audience members may be annoyed if a speech has a drastically different tone from the one they were expecting. For instance, an audience expecting a serious speech will be impatient with a speaker who spends a great deal of time trying to make them laugh. In some cases, it may be necessary to thwart the expectations of the audience, as for instance when a serious moral point must be made instead of providing sheer entertainment.

Importance of tailoring the subject of a speech to the qualifications of the audience: When deciding upon the subject matter of a speech, the speaker should take into account the audience's general intelligence level and the subject-related knowledge. A speech will be ineffective if it is either too elementary or too advanced for the audience. If the speaker is unfamiliar with the knowledge base of the proposed audience, he or she should take steps to determine this knowledge before preparing the speech. For an unschooled audience, it is a good idea to focus on the most basic and important principles of a given subject. For an audience of experts in a given field, however, it is important to provide information that will be stimulating and informative.

Importance of defining the purpose of the speech: In preparation for making a speech, it is important to must strictly define the purpose of the speech. Without a firm idea of the intention of the speech, it will be too easy for the content to miss the mark. To begin with, the speaker should consider his or her own intentions as well as the intentions of the audience. As much as possible, the intentions of the speaker and those of the audience should be made to overlap. One should define the central argument or idea to be expressed in the speech and take care that this argument or idea is consistent with the intention of the speech. It is also important that the title of the speech indicates the intention as well as the central theme of the speech.

Difference between an idea and a claim in a speech: The goal of a speech is to disseminate information or persuade the audience. In other words, a speaker will either deliver ideas or make claims. A speaker who is delivering ideas is expressing information and opinions for their own sake, and not necessarily trying to change the minds of the audience. Informative speeches are usually on subjects about which the audience is not expected to know very much. The purpose of such a speech is to increase the knowledge of the audience rather than to convert them to any particular viewpoint. When a speaker makes claims, on the other hand, he or she is introducing opinions that may or may not be held by the members of the audience. The intention of this type of speech will be to provide arguments and evidence to support the speaker's claims.

Process of Phrasing the Main Idea of the Speech

It is important when giving an informative speech to lay out the main idea in a manner comprehensible to the audience. The main idea of an informative speech should be presented near the beginning of the address and therefore should not require an audience to understand any concepts that will be explained later in the speech. The audience should be able to understand the gist of the main idea before the speaker goes on to elaborate. In the preparation of a speech, the speaker should define the main idea early on, so that he or she can procure evidence and supporting arguments appropriate to that main idea. Too often, speakers introduce evidence and arguments not directly supportive of the main idea of the speech. This causes confusion among the audience and waters down the effect of the speech.

Process of Phrasing the Main Claim in a Speech

When a speech is designed to present or advance a particular viewpoint, the speaker will need to pay special attention to the phrasing of the speech's main claim. The main claim should be phrased in such a way that it will be comprehensible to a general audience and will not offend casual listeners with a harsh or controversial tone. The degree of intensity appropriate to the claim will depend on the audience. A more strident tone can be used with an audience of like-minded individuals, whereas a diverse group of uncommitted listeners requires a more evenhanded tone. When constructing the main claim of a speech, the speaker should be sure to present only ideas that can be supported by available evidence and reasonable argument. If the main claim of a speech is far-fetched or unsupportable, even the more rational elements of the speech may be dismissed by a skeptical audience.

Fundamental Qualities of a Well-Organized Speech

All well-organized speeches have certain qualities in common. For instance, a well-organized speech is comprehensible, meaning it can be understood by all members of the audience. A well-organized speech also has a formal unity, which means all of its parts contribute to the main idea. A unified speech has no extraneous parts. A well-organized speech is also comprehensive—it covers all the issues an audience member would expect to be addressed by a speech on the given subject. Finally, a well-organized speech does not have any repetition. Every major point should be covered in its entirety, but no points need to be repeated once they have been clearly delivered.

Process of Speech Organization

The process of speech organization entails selecting the elements that will comprise the speech, placing them into a coherent order, and arranging the supporting material for each message unit. During the organization process, a speaker will often summarize each message unit in a simple sentence. This gives the speaker simple building blocks that can be easily rearranged. In general, a speech should include a coherent introduction, body, and conclusion. The introduction should engage the interest of the audience and summarize the main points to be made. The body should contain the central points of the speaker's argument, as well as the supporting evidence. The conclusion should summarize the argument and give the audience food for thought.

Outline for a Proof Speech

Speech communication instructors often refer to a "proof speech." This is a common type of speech, in which the speaker introduces his or her argument and then attempts to prove it. Proof speeches follow a consistent pattern. In brief, a proof speech has four components: introduction, argument, development, and conclusion. A speech that follows this pattern allows the audience to become acquainted with the thrust of the speaker's arguments before substantiation is offered. The lengths of the various components of a proof speech will vary, depending on the speaker's interests and the knowledge level of the audience. For instance, an audience already familiar with the subject matter may not require as much supporting material to be convinced.

Impromptu Speech Pattern

Any relatively informal speech on a light subject can be referred to as an impromptu speech. An impromptu speech may be given on very short notice and will therefore give evidence of much less preparation. Even so, impromptu speeches tend to follow a similar pattern. There are four basic steps in a typical impromptu speech: an engaging introduction, a brief overview, elaboration, and summary. Notice that the four components of an impromptu speech directly parallel the components of a proof speech. The only real difference is that the delivery will be looser and the style of delivery will endeavor to be more entertaining. An impromptu speech often begins with a humorous or intriguing anecdote and often ends with a light touch as well.

Problem-Solving Pattern of Speech-Making

In a problem-solving speech, the speaker outlines a particular problem, attempts to diagnose the cause, and then suggests a potential solution. Problem-solving speeches are at their heart persuasive speeches, since they attempt to convince the audience of the merits of adopting a particular strategy to solve a given problem. To be effective, however, a problem-solving speech needs to follow a logical pattern. These speeches typically begin with an introduction and a definition of the problem in question. The speaker will then summarize the possible causes of the problem and discuss some of the possible solutions. Following this, the speaker will make a case for one of the solutions and provide supporting evidence and argumentation. Finally, the speaker will attempt to rebut some of the possible counterarguments to the proposed solution.

Appropriate Outline for a Call-to-Action Speech

When speech communication instructors describe a call-to-action speech, they are referring to a speech that intends to inspire the audience to follow some recommended course of action. A call-to-action speech has five typical components: engaging the audience, describing why the audience should want to change something, explaining the best way to change, describing the positive consequences of making the change, and directly indicating how change can be made. It is not really possible to rearrange the steps in a call-to-action speech. Unless the argument is delivered in this order, the speech will likely be ineffective. It is important to end by outlining the positive consequences of change and making an emotional plea, as this leaves the audience on a high note, which is most likely to translate into direct action.

Body Language in Public Speaking

Posture in Public Speaking

Many speakers fail to recognize the significance of proper posture in the delivery of a speech. As much as words or gestures, a speaker's posture transmits information about his or her attitude, credibility, and confidence. To present a message effectively, a speaker should stand up as straight and tall as possible. Slouching forward or bending over one's notes indicates a lack of interest and preparation. This kind of advice may seem trivial, but an audience will subconsciously pay closer attention to anyone whose posture indicates command and authority. Effective speakers pay close attention to their own posture and make sure that poor posture does not disrupt the transmission of their message.

Facial Expression in Public Speaking

The facial expressions made by a speaker can have a significant impact on the effectiveness of message delivery. The facial expressions of the speaker can either reinforce or contradict his or her words. If the words being spoken are amusing or colorful, it is appropriate for the speaker to be smiling and have a relaxed facial expression. If the speaker is addressing a serious subject while grinning, however, the audience will most likely discount what he or she is saying. A speaker needs to match his or her facial expressions to the subject matter and to the expectations of the audience. A large audience can expect the facial expressions of the speaker to be slightly exaggerated, while a small audience may be put off by what seems like a leering or grimacing speaker.

Eye Contact in Public Speaking

Speakers should never underestimate the importance of eye contact during message delivery. For one thing, it is very difficult for an audience member who is making eye contact with the speaker to lose interest. An effective speaker will often shift his or her gaze around the room, making eye contact with as many people as possible. Under no circumstances should a speaker look up in the air, stare at his or her notes, or fix his or her eyes on some point in the distance. At the same time, the speaker should not constantly move his or her eyes around the room, as this may be perceived as anxious behavior. Eye movements should be calm, regular, and smooth.

Gestures in Public Speaking

A public speaker should make sure that his or her gestures are in harmony with the subject matter of the speech and the expectations of the audience. Many people are in the habit of either moving their hands frequently during speech or keeping their hands stationary. Both of these approaches are only appropriate in certain circumstances. When delivering a speech to a large audience, or delivering a speech with a high emotional content, a speaker may be advised to incorporate wide, energetic gestures. These kinds of motions are not appropriate for a more somber subject, however. And although gestures can amplify the meaning of the speaker's words, they should never become a distraction from the message of the speech.

Proper Way to Use Notes During a Speech

Many speakers will require notes, but they should rely on these notes as little as possible during delivery of the speech. For one thing, notes tend to prevent a speaker from making effective eye contact and using his or her hands expressively while speaking. Also, speakers who become reliant on notes may not be able to orient themselves in a speech if something goes wrong with the notes. Notes should only be used as a reference point of last resort. They should be kept down in front of the speaker, preferably out of view of the audience. They should not be held and should be on as few pieces of paper as possible, to prevent excessive shuffling during a speech. Finally, a speaker who requires notes should carefully look them over before a speech to make sure they are understandable and arranged properly.

Skills Required for Making a Speech

To deliver a successful speech, an individual needs to have acquired certain skills. For one thing, the speaker must understand in depth the topic about which he or she is speaking. He or she must also be able to address the topic from a number of different points of view and to answer any questions the audience might have after the speech. More generally, a successful speaker must have an air of authority, so the audience will pay attention and trust his or her words. A speaker should also have what is known as rhetorical sensitivity, or the ability to adapt his or her message to different audiences. Successful speakers know that a given style of speaking may be very effective with one audience and ineffective with another. A successful speaker will be able to modulate his or her voice and gestures appropriately.

State Apprehension as a Component of Speech Anxiety

To some extent, everyone grapples with speech anxiety. The fear of embarrassment or public disclosure can be overcome only with significant practice at public speaking. There are a couple of different kinds of speech anxiety. "State apprehension" is defined as speech anxiety that is only felt in specific situations. For instance, an individual who is comfortable talking in class but becomes anxious when required to speak informally with peers is experiencing state apprehension. Many people experience state apprehension in relation to delivering formal speeches in front of a group. State apprehension has both physical and mental symptoms, including vocal tics, sweaty palms, and a trembling voice.

Trait Apprehension as a Component of Speech Anxiety

Some people experience speech anxiety to a greater degree than others. Those aspects of speech anxiety that are unique to an individual are known as trait apprehensions. For instance, someone might have an aversion to public speaking because of a past experience. People who have an unnaturally high level of trait apprehension tend to avoid situations in which they will be required to speak to a large group. The good news for these individuals is that trait apprehension can be overcome with experience. Unfortunately, however, this means practicing public speaking until it becomes natural.

Interpretation of Speech Anxiety

Speech anxiety is a common malady but not one that should cause a person to lose heart. Even the most successful speakers have a bit of anxiety when delivering a message. In a way, this anxiety is a positive thing, because it focuses the attention and encourages concentration. Speech anxiety is a natural response to confronting an uncertain and unfamiliar situation. Research suggests that those who suffer from severe speech anxiety are often the most effective public speakers. Also, most speakers report that the anxiety they feel before delivering a speech is much greater than the anxiety they feel when actually in the process of speaking.

Using Speech Anxiety Productively

The abundance of nervous energy felt before delivering a speech can be used to the speaker's advantage. For one thing, many people find that speech anxiety sharpens their senses and focuses their concentration on the task at hand. Human beings are naturally inclined to focus their attention when they perceive a threat. The good thing about speech anxiety is that the attention is sharpened even though the threat is not significant. Many accomplished speakers use speech anxiety to increase their level of excitement and dynamism while delivering a speech. Indeed, many speakers say that without speech anxiety, they would not be able to achieve the rhetorical effects that have made them successful speakers.

Four Basic Channels of Public Communication

Normally, speech delivery is considered a simple transmission of words by one person to a group. However, this is only one of the channels through which information is delivered during a speech. In the technical language of speech communication, the speaker's words are said to pass through the verbal channel. At the same time, the speaker's tone of voice indicates his or her attitude through the aural channel. Some speakers use visual aids, which transmit information through the pictorial channel. Finally, a speaker transmits information about his or her attitude and self-image through gestures and facial expressions. This transmission is said to pass through the visual channel.

Importance of Physical Setting in the Delivery of a Speech

The physical setting in which a speech is delivered exerts significant influence over the expectations of the audience and should therefore be taken into account by the speaker beforehand. For instance, an audience that is required to stand during a speech will have less patience for a long-winded and complex oration. On the other hand, if the audience is seated in soft, plush chairs, they may be too relaxed to pay attention to a serious lecture. When the subject of a speech requires a fair amount of technical detail, it is a good idea for the audience to be seated in upright chairs and for the room to have sufficient light. In any case, the speaker should consider how physical setting will influence the mood of the audience and should adjust his or her speech accordingly.

How Social Context Can Influence the Delivery of a Speech

When speakers consider the characteristics of the environment in which they will deliver their speech, they sometimes neglect to consider the social context. The social context is the set of relationships between the members of the audience and the speaker and between the members of the audience themselves. The speaker should know beforehand how he or she stands in relation to the audience. For instance, a speaker may be recognized as an expert, an entertainer, or an intriguing fraud. Also, the speaker should understand how the members of the audience stand in relation to one another; whether they are friends, colleagues, or strangers, for instance. The information gained by this consideration of social context should inform the construction and delivery of the speech.

How Communication Rules Can Influence the Delivery of a Speech

Sometimes a speech will be delivered in a particular environment or to a particular group that is governed by specific communication rules. For instance, a speech delivered in church is unlikely to be followed by a question-and-answer period. As another example, some debating societies have strict rules for the presentation and critique of a speech. In more informal situations, some groups will have different expectations for speaker behavior For instance; a gathering of senior citizens is unlikely to respond well to coarse humor. In other words, communication rules may be explicit or implicit. While preparing a speech, the speaker needs to address the formal considerations that will influence his or her message.

Principles of Argumentation and Debate

Basics of a Formal Debate

A debate is simply an organized communication event in which two or more parties offer opposing views on the same subject. A debate is not a synonym for an argument. Debates are meant to be civil and constructive. A typical debate format has two sides: affirmative and negative. A statement known as a proposition is read and the affirmative side argues in favor of it. The negative side then argues against it. It should be noted that the hosting sides of the debate are not trying to persuade one another, but rather are trying to convince some third party, whether it is a judge or the audience. The terms of the debate are usually set ahead of time. These may include time limits and order of speaking.

Characteristics of a Good Proposition

In a debate, the statement to be discussed is called the proposition. Some propositions are better than others at inspiring good debate. A proposition that has an obvious answer, for instance, will not be very good for debate because one side of the argument will be much stronger than the other. A proposition should be limited to a reasonable scope of application, so that the debaters can focus on a few key issues. Also, the wording of the proposition should be simple and clear. The debate should be centered on the topic indicated by the proposition and not on the meaning of the words in the proposition.

Propositions of Value in Formal Debates

In a formal debate, propositions begin with the words "resolved that" followed by the statement. There are three basic kinds of proposition: propositions of value, propositions of judgment, and propositions of policy. A proposition of value makes a statement about the correctness or practical utility of something. For instance, a proposition of value might state that eliminating summer vacation in favor of year-round schooling is a good idea. The affirmative position will then argue in favor of this proposition and the negative position will argue against it. Propositions of value usually require statistical evidence to be supported or opposed effectively.

Propositions of Judgment in Formal Debates

In a formal debate, propositions begin with the words "resolved that" followed by the statement. There are three basic kinds of proposition: propositions of value, propositions of judgment, and propositions of policy. A proposition of judgment states that something is true or exists. For this reason, propositions of judgment are often referred to as propositions of fact. For instance, a proposition of judgment might state that men generally earn more money for the same labor than do women. This is an unfortunate fact, and it will be up to the affirmative position to provide the argument proving it to be so.

Propositions of Policy in Formal Debates

In a formal debate, propositions begin with the words "resolved that" followed by the statement. There are three basic kinds of proposition: propositions of value, propositions of judgment, and propositions of policy. A proposition of policy declares that a particular course of action should be taken. Propositions of policy usually include the words "ought" or "should." For instance, a proposition of policy might read: "resolved, that teachers should be required to eat lunch with their classes." Propositions of policy often make for the liveliest debate because there is no way of absolutely knowing whether a proposed policy will be effective.

Process of Finding a Debate Topic

The first step in the planning of a debate is to find an appropriate topic, or issue. The best issues are those that are controversial without being potentially offensive and which provide equal opportunity for both sides to make a convincing case. Of course, the responsibility of proving a proposition is borne by the affirmative side. Debate instructors have isolated three common issues in a policy proposition debate. First, the debaters will need to determine whether there is a pressing need for immediate change. They will also have to decide whether there is a plan that provides the appropriate change. Finally, the affirmative side will have to prove that the proposed plan is the best available plan. The negative side is not required to win all three of these issues, but the affirmative side is required to win all three in order to hold sway.

Defining Terms in a Debate

For a debate to be successful, any unclear or abstract terms must be defined at the appropriate time. Debates are not meant to be inquiries into the meaning of the words in the proposition. Rather, the propositions should be clear enough to be understood without a problem by both the affirmative and negative sides. If the proposition includes any troublesome language, it is usually the responsibility of the first speaker in the debate to define the terms. Since the affirmative speaker is the one who is responsible for proving his or her case, it makes sense for him or her to define the terms of the proposition.

Constructing Debate Cases

The process of constructing a debate case is very similar to constructing an outline for a speech. It is common for both sides in the debate to compose what is known as a debate brief, in which their case is outlined point by point. These debate briefs are prepared ahead of time; as the debate proceeds, each side will outline the argument made by the other side in what is known as a flow sheet. A debate brief usually begins with a thesis statement and, if necessary, definitions for any problematic terms in the proposition. It then goes on to list the major points to be made as well as rebuttals to potential counter-arguments made by the other side.

Finding Proof in a Debate

The ability of either side in a debate to claim victory will depend on its ability to produce adequate proof. In a debate, proof consists of two basic components: evidence and reasoning. Evidence is factual information. Reasoning, on the other hand, is the set of inferences or judgments drawn from evidence. To provide adequate proof, then, a debater will need to have both evidence and reasoning. The debater must also have this information organized so that he or she can use it to greatest effect during the course of the debate and so it can be produced in direct contrast to the argument made by the opposing side.

Evidence as It is Used in a Debate

In a debate, evidence is the factual information used to support an argument. To be successful, a debater must have substantial evidence to support his or her case. It is a good idea to record this information on paper before the beginning of the debate. The most important pieces of evidence should be used in the first speech made by each side, known as the constructive speech. As a debate progresses, minor pieces of evidence can be used in the various rebuttal speeches. Also, a debater should recognize which evidence is appropriate for supporting his or her main case and which evidence is better suited to rebut possible counterarguments by the opponent. Debaters should be able to identify the sources of their evidence.

Common Tests of Evidence for a Debate

During preparation for a debate, each side will gather as much evidence as possible to support their case. They will need to apply strict guidelines in their evidence-gathering in order to make sure they only select evidence that will stand up to their opponent's scrutiny. The four most important qualities of good evidence are relevance, consistency, timeliness, and the ability to be verified. A piece of evidence needs to pertain directly to the argument being made. It needs to hold up in a number of different conditions and be the same from different sources. It needs to have been produced recently enough to remain believable. Finally, it needs to be susceptible to verification so that the debate judge does not have to depend on the word of the debater.

Common Kinds of Evidence Used in a Debate

A few different kinds of evidence are commonly used in debates. Perhaps the most common form of evidence is documented statistics. Statistics can be obtained from a variety of books, trade journals, and other publications. Sometimes debaters will introduce the testimony or writings of acknowledged authorities on the subject. It is important to establish the credentials of the authority when this kind of evidence is used. Finally, debaters will often rely upon what they believe to be commonly accepted facts. These are matters of truth generally accepted by a reasonable audience and therefore do not need further support.

Inductive Reasoning in a Debate

Debaters frequently rely upon inductive reasoning in making their points. Inductive reasoning is the process of beginning with a group of specifics and gradually working toward a general idea. In other words, inductive reasoning begins by looking at the trees and eventually broadens the scope to take in the whole forest. For instance, someone debating from the affirmative view might begin by citing a number of statistics. He or she could then make a general point that is supported by all those statistics. Inductive reasoning is a good way to utilize pieces of evidence that can stand alone.

Deductive Reasoning in a Debate

In the process of deductive reasoning, a debater transitions from a general rule to a specific instance of the rule. The debater first offers what is known as a premise. For example, a premise might be "All teachers love summer vacation." The debater will then offer an example of this premise in what is known as the minor premise: "We are all teachers." The debater will then give the conclusion that stems from the information so far provided: "We love summer vacation." This process is known as a logical syllogism. For a syllogism to be logically correct, all of the premises must be true. This example of deductive reasoning, then, would be easy to argue against, since there are probably teachers who do not love summer vacation.

Refutation in a Debate

The negative side in the debate is primarily responsible for refutation, or the act of damaging the opponent's case. The process of refutation has a few general components. First, the argument to be refuted is defined. Next, the importance that this argument has to the opponent is emphasized. The debater then presents his or her counterargument, along with evidence in support of it. Finally, the debater summarizes his or her refutation and makes any necessary clarifications. Refutation does not necessarily need to constitute a direct attack on the opponent's position. Instead, it is possible to refute an opponent's argument by simply offering a stronger argument for one's own side.

Rebuttal in a Debate

The process of rebuttal is a formal element in a debate. A rebuttal gives the debater an opportunity to counter any refutation of his or her argument that has just been made during a rebuttal; the debater is allowed to introduce new evidence but may not make a new argument. To begin a rebuttal, the debater will restate the arguments that have been made so far. The debater will then restate the refutation offered by the other side. Then, the debater will attempt to demonstrate problems with the opponent's arguments. He or she will then give any additional information to strengthen his position and will conclude by summarizing his or her original argument.

Traditional Form of Debate

In a traditional debate, also known as a standard debate, there are two sides composed of two individuals. The affirmative side speaks first and the negative side speaks second. A traditional debate generally lasts for about an hour and begins with a ten- minute speech by the first affirmative speaker. This is followed by a five-minute rebuttal from the first negative speaker. The first negative speaker is then given ten minutes to make a constructive speech, followed by a five-minute rebuttal from the first affirmative speaker. This arrangement is then duplicated with the second members of each team.

Cross-Examination Form of Debate

In a cross-examination debate, the affirmative side and the negative side both have two members. Unlike in a traditional debate, where debaters are given lengthy amounts of time in which to make their cases and counter-arguments, a cross-examination debate encourages each side to directly question the other. It begins with a constructive speech by the first affirmative speaker, followed by a few minutes in which the second negative speaker can question the first speaker. The first negative speaker then makes a constructive speech, followed by a few minutes of questioning from the first affirmative speaker. The second affirmative speaker then delivers a message, followed by questioning from the first negative speaker. The second negative speaker delivers a message and is then questioned by the second affirmative speaker. The first negative speaker issues a rebuttal speech, followed by a rebuttal speech from the first affirmative speaker. Finally, the second negative speaker issues a rebuttal, concluding with a rebuttal from the second affirmative speaker.

Lincoln-Douglas Form of Debate

The common format for a two-person debate is typically referred to as a **Lincoln-Douglas debate**, in reference to the celebrated debates between Abraham Lincoln and Stephen A. Douglas in Illinois in 1858. In the contemporary arrangement, the debate begins with a topic being introduced by the moderator. The affirmative speaker then has six minutes to deliver his or her constructive, followed by a three-minute cross examination from the negative speaker. The negative speaker is then given seven minutes to deliver their negative construction (which almost always include a negative rebuttal), followed by a three-minute cross examination from the affirmative speaker. The affirmative speaker is then given four minutes to issue a rebuttal and is then followed by a six-minute rebuttal from the negative speaker. The affirmative speaker then concludes with a final three-minute rebuttal. Lincoln Douglas debates often end with the floor being opened to questions from the audience.

First Affirmative Constructive Speech in a Traditional Debate

In a traditional debate, the first affirmative constructive speech should be the only one that can be fully organized ahead of time. It is during this speech that the main argument of the affirmative side is advanced. The speaker should also clear up any problems with language that may exist in the proposition and deliver any important background information required to understand the topic. The speaker will then outline the major points of the affirmative case and will give as much evidence as possible within the time constraints. At the conclusion of the first affirmative constructive speech, the speaker will summarize his or her main argument.

First Negative Constructive Speaker in a Traditional Debate

After the first affirmative constructive speech has been made in a traditional debate, the first negative constructive speech will be given. In this speech, the negative speaker issues his or her basic response to the arguments advanced by the affirmative side. He or she may call into question the definitions offered by the affirmative side. For the most part, however, the first negative constructive speaker is likely to attack the premises and evidence given by the first affirmative speaker. If appropriate, the first negative constructive speaker may want to advance an alternative to the argument proposed by the first speaker.

Second Affirmative Constructive Speech in a Traditional Debate

In a traditional debate, the second affirmative constructive speech follows the first negative constructive speech. In this speech, the affirmative speaker directly addresses the counter-arguments made by the first negative constructive speaker. The affirmative speaker may wish to clarify any problems that have been raised about the language in the proposition. The affirmative speaker should address all the counter-arguments made by the first negative constructive speaker. It is best to address these points in a systematic manner.

Second Negative Constructive Speech in a Traditional Debate

In a traditional debate, the second negative constructive speech follows the second affirmative constructive speech. The second negative constructive speech is a brief period in which the negative speaker can summarize the debate to this point strengthen his or her own case, and then attack the major arguments of the second affirmative speech. This is the final constructive speech in the debate, so the second negative speaker will want to make every argument he or she has available since new arguments will not be allowed in the rebuttal sections. It is a good idea to conclude the second negative constructive speech with a simple but forceful counter-argument to the affirmative case.

Contributions of the First Negative Rebuttal Speech and the First Affirmative Rebuttal Speech in a Traditional Debate

The second negative constructive speech is the final constructive speech in a traditional debate. At this point, the rebuttal speeches begin. The first negative rebuttal speech serves as a reminder of the major weaknesses in the affirmative case. The first negative rebuttal speaker will also take this opportunity to re-state the arguments made by the negative side. Next, the first affirmative rebuttal will review the high points of the affirmative case and will attempt to counter any arguments that were made during the first negative rebuttal. The first affirmative rebuttal speech will also include a response to the second negative constructive speech.

Contributions of the Second Negative Rebuttal Speech and the Second Affirmative Rebuttal Speech in a Traditional Debate

The arguments made by the negative side in a traditional debate will conclude with the second negative rebuttal speech. In this speech, the negative side will conclude their argument, resolving any questions about their side, and pleading with the debate judges to agree with their point of view. A traditional debate concludes with the second affirmative rebuttal speech. In this speech, the affirmative side summarizes their argument and response to the previous rebuttal speech. Finally, the affirmative side delivers their own plea for the support of the debate judges. These judges may be specially chosen or may simply be the audience at the event.

Purpose of Parliamentary Procedure During Meetings

Parliamentary procedure is a system of administrating meetings. These rules were developed for formal situations, but they are often used by informal organizations to keep business on track and provide structure to professional interactions. One of the benefits of parliamentary procedure is that it gives every member of a group an opportunity to participate in making proposals and voting. Also, parliamentary procedure limits the control that can be exercised by any person or group of people and therefore makes decision-making a more streamlined process. Parliamentary procedure can be used by very large and very small organizations.

Following terms related to parliamentary procedure: abstain, amend, chair, floor, majority, and minority.

Parliamentary procedure has its own set of terms, which include:

- Abstain: to opt not to vote on a particular proposal.
- Amend: to change the words in a particular proposal.
- Chair: the person who is designated to preside over the activities of the group.
- Floor: the authority to speak.
- Majority: the position supported by a larger group of people; in parliamentary procedure, the majority holds more influence than the minority.
- Minority: the position supported by a smaller group of people; certain rights of the minority are guaranteed by parliamentary procedure.
- Following terms related to parliamentary procedure: minutes, motion, pending, second, and table. Parliamentary procedure has its own set of terms, which include:
    - Minutes: the written report of the happenings at the previous meeting.
    - Motion: a proposal that the group will consider.
    - Pending: in the process of being considered, as in "the motion is pending".

- Second: approve a motion publicly; to be introduced for discussion, a proposal must be seconded.
- Table: set aside a motion until a later time; this is done when more information is likely to be obtained, at which point it will become more appropriate to discuss the given motion.

"Majority rules" principle of parliamentary procedure: In parliamentary procedure, decisions are made on a democratic basis. In other words, the will of the majority drives the decision-making process. The success of an organization relies on the ability of the minority to accept the decisions of the majority. In parliamentary procedure, a simple majority is defined as any more than one half of the voting individuals. Those who do not vote (that is, who abstain from voting) are not counted in the calculation of simple majority. For important decisions, an organization might require a two-thirds majority vote, as this means the decision will require a greater consensus in order to be made.

Rights of the Minority in Parliamentary Procedure

Although the decisions made within the framework of parliamentary procedure favor the majority, the minority is accorded certain rights. Within parliamentary procedure, there are numerous opportunities for the members of the minority to make their voices heard in an attempt to persuade other members of the group. Even after a decision has been made, the minority is given a chance to declare its sentiments. Moreover, the chairperson is responsible for not favoring or showing undue influence on behalf of the majority. One of the resulting benefits of parliamentary procedure is that no one becomes alienated or feels excluded from the process.

Principle of Equal Rights and Responsibilities in Parliamentary Procedure

In parliamentary procedure, all members of the organization are given equal rights in all responsibilities. Certain members of the organization may be designated as leaders or may be given other special roles, but this is only done with the consent of all the members. Within a parliamentary organization, every member is given the right to vote and the right to speak his or her mind. It should be noted, however, that parliamentary procedure frames these actions as responsibilities as well as rights. That is, in order for an organization to be healthy, all of the members need to participate by voting and making their opinions known.

Emphasis on Discussing One Problem at a Time in Parliamentary Procedure

One of the things that parliamentary procedure emphasizes is that discussion should be organized in order to minimize digressions and confusion. It is the job of the chairperson to introduce issues to the group and to make clear transitions between discussion topics. The most important issues before the group should always be discussed first. Usually, an issue will be discussed for a limited amount of time, at which point the group will decide whether to vote on it. It is only after a vote has been held or the issue has been tabled that the group can move on to the next issue. The best chairpersons are those who limit discussion to the matter at hand and efficiently move through the agenda of the group.

Emphasis on Maintaining Focus in Parliamentary Procedure

For a parliamentary organization to function effectively, the members need to limit their discussion to the issues currently on the floor. In part, this is the responsibility of the chairperson, but each member needs to be careful to limit his or her speech to the issues at hand. Every motion requires a second in order to be discussed. If some members of the group feel that discussion has gone on too long, they may call for a two-thirds vote to end discussion and hold a vote. If they do not achieve the two-thirds majority, discussion may continue. A chairperson can cut members off if they begin to speak on subjects other than those on the floor.

Chair's Objectivity in Parliamentary Procedure

To administer a parliamentary organization in a fair manner, a chairperson must remain objective at all times. A chairperson cannot be seen to favor either side in the debate. This is especially important because the opinions of the chairperson have the ability to sway the opinion of the members. The important consideration for members, however, should be the quality of the arguments on either side and not the opinions of the chairperson. In order to be viewed as objective, a chairperson needs to allow equal time to both sides.

Parliamentary Procedure

Following elements of the order of business in parliamentary procedure: finding the quorum, call to order, and reading of the minutes. Parliamentary procedure outlines a specific order of business. First, a certain number of members must be in attendance before business can be introduced. This minimum number of members, which is usually one more than half of the total members, is referred to as a quorum. Once a quorum has been reached, the chair will call the meeting to order. At this point, the meeting has begun. The secretary will then read the minutes from the last meeting. After the minutes have been read, the chair will ask if any members of the group have any additions or corrections to make to the minutes. If not, the minutes will be approved.

Officer reports, unfinished business, and new business. After the minutes have been approved, the group may hear from various officers who serve as committee heads. For instance, the treasurer often makes a report at this point in the meeting. An organization may have standing committees, which exist in perpetuity, or special committees, which are created to accomplish specific purposes and disbanded after the purpose is accomplished. Once the committees have reported, the chair will ask if there is any unfinished business in front of the group. If there is, it must be resolved before moving on. Once unfinished business is complete, the chair will open the floor to new business. Upon opening the floor to new business, the chair may briefly describe the agenda for the current meeting. The chair may also ask if any member of the group has items to be added to the agenda. At this point, members of the group can propose motions.

Parliamentary procedure: announcements, adjournments, and voting. It is during the introduction of new business that elections for new officers in the group are held. The chair will call for nominations and seconds and then voting will occur. After new business is complete, the chair may ask the group if they have any particular announcements to make. After all business is complete, the chair may ask if there is a motion to adjourn. If so, the group can vote on whether or not to end the meeting.

Various kinds of voting that take place in parliamentary procedure. According to parliamentary procedure, voting can take place in a number of different ways. The most common form of vote is a voice vote, in which all those in favor of the motion say "aye" and all those opposed to the motion say "nay." Voting can also be held by having members stand up or raise their hands to indicate their approval or disapproval of a motion. In a roll call vote, the names of the members of a group are called out loud one by one and each member indicates his or her vote. Finally, a secret ballot can be held when members prefer anonymity.

Types of Motions Made According to Parliamentary Procedure

Main Motions and Subsidiary Motions

According to parliamentary procedure, a motion can be made in a number of different ways. A main motion is use to introduce the topic for discussion. If a main motion gets a second, the motion will be discussed and will require a majority vote for passage. A subsidiary motion, on the other hand, is introduced to alter or eliminate some other motion. Subsidiary motions are issued after a main motion. They must be voted on before the attention of the group can return to the main motion. Subsidiary motions include the motion to table, to postpone debate, or to amend the main motion.

Privileged motions, incidental motions, and unclassified motions: According to parliamentary procedure, a motion can be made in a number of different ways. A privileged motion has to do with the requirements of the members. For instance, a privileged motion may be made to adjourn at a certain time or to set a date for a future meeting. An incidental motion has to do with the way business is conducted in the meeting. An incidental motion may be made to withdraw a motion, for instance, or to object to a certain idea. Incidental motions refine motions that have already been made. Finally, an unclassified motion attempts to recall issues that have been tabled or dismissed earlier.

Motion to fix time to reassemble: In parliamentary procedure, a motion to fix time to reassemble is a privileged motion. Indeed, in the table of motions used in parliamentary procedure, it is the most privileged motion, meaning that it is more important than any other motion. This motion is typically made directly after a motion to adjourn has been seconded. It is made, however, before the motion to adjourn has been voted on. This is because the motion to adjourn will then be voted on taking into account the proposed time for future meetings. No debate takes place on a motion to fix time to reassemble, although the motion may be amended. A simple majority is required to pass this motion.

Motion to adjourn: In parliamentary procedure, a motion to adjourn is the privileged motion that usually ends a meeting. If some members of a group feel that debate has gone on too long, or if they do not like the way the debate is tending, they may call a motion to adjourn as a way of stopping discussion, if the motion is seconded, it must be voted on immediately. A motion to adjourn requires a simple majority. It is not debatable or amendable. It should be noted that a motion to adjourn does not eliminate the subject under discussion for good; on the contrary, because the issue under discussion has not been resolved, it will be taken up again at the next meeting.

Motion to recess: In parliamentary procedure, a motion to recess is a privileged motion in which one member moves to suspend a meeting for a brief period of time without fully ending it. For instance, a member might make a motion to recess for lunch. One of the advantages of going into recess rather than adjourning a meeting is that after a recess, the regular order of business does not need to be repeated. This can save a great deal of time. A motion to recess requires a second and is debatable and amendable. It requires a simple majority for passage.

Motion to rise to a question of privilege: In parliamentary procedure, a motion to rise to a question of privilege is a privileged motion in which a member asks permission to make a request regarding the safety, comfort, and convenience of the group. In other words, this is a motion that briefly interrupts discussion to take care of some environmental distraction. For instance, a member might make a motion for a question of privilege if he or she wants to adjust the air-conditioning in the meeting room. The passage of this kind of motion simply depends on the will of the chairperson. A motion to rise to a question of privilege does not require a second and is neither debatable nor amendable.

Motion to call for the orders of the day: In parliamentary procedure, a motion to call for the orders of the day is a privileged motion in which a member asks that attention be paid to the predetermined order of business in a meeting. This kind of motion is typically made when a member feels that the agreed-upon order has been abandoned or that the group has forgotten its original intent in a discussion. A motion to call for the orders of the day can interrupt a speaker and does not require a second. It is neither debatable nor amendable. The chairperson decides whether or not this motion will be passed.

Motion to appeal a decision: A motion to appeal the decision in parliamentary procedure is an incidental motion in which a member disagrees with the decision made by the chair and asks for a vote of all the members. This motion is typically made after a motion decided solely by the chairperson. It is debatable but not amendable. Before voting on this motion, both sides are allowed to briefly state their cases. It is acceptable to interrupt a speaker with this motion, but the motion requires a second in order to come to a vote. For passage, this motion requires a simple majority.

Motion to rise to a point of order: In parliamentary procedure, a motion to rise to a point of order is an incidental motion in which a member seeks to indicate that a procedural error has been made. A member might make this motion if he or she feels that discussion has wandered off-topic or that the order of business has not been followed. A member may interrupt discussion to make this motion and it does not require a second. A motion to rise to a point of order is neither debatable nor amendable. Its passage depends on the will of the chairperson.

Motion to call for a division of the assembly: In parliamentary procedure, a motion to call for a division of the assembly is an incidental motion in which a member declares that a voice vote has been too close to call and that a more precise vote should be taken. Specifically, a motion for a division of the assembly calls for a vote by show of hands or by standing. This motion may be made as an interruption to current discussion and does not require a second. It is neither debatable nor amendable. A motion to call for a division of the assembly requires a simple majority for passage.

Motion to object to a consideration of a question: In parliamentary procedure, a motion to object to a consideration of a question is an incidental motion used to stop discussion of a particular topic. This motion may be made for any number of reasons. In some cases, a member may feel that the discussion is fruitless or that it has wandered too far away from the original topic. A member might also feel that the meeting has run on too long. A motion to object to consideration of a question can be made as an interruption to discussion and does not require a second. It is not debatable or amendable. Because it is such an important motion, in that it has the ability to stop discussion, it requires a two-thirds majority.

Motion to ask permission to withdraw a motion: In parliamentary procedure, a motion to ask permission to withdraw a motion is an incidental motion in which a member tries to remove a motion that has been previously made. For instance, a motion might seem like a good idea at the time but after subsequent discussion may be discovered to be weak or wrongheaded. In such a case, the member who made the motion may ask permission to withdraw it. A motion to ask permission to withdraw a motion cannot interrupt a speaker and does not require a second. It is neither debatable nor amendable. It requires a simple majority for passage.

Motion to suspend a rule: In parliamentary procedure, a motion to suspend a rule is an incidental motion used when a group wants to temporarily remove the restrictions placed on it by a certain rule. For instance, in some cases it might be appropriate to alter the normal order of business in order to obtain an important piece of information from a committee report. A member could then move to suspend that rule in this particular case. This motion cannot be made as an interruption to a speaker and it requires a second. It is neither debatable nor amendable. Because it calls for a fundamental change in the rules of the group, this motion requires a two-thirds majority for passage.

Motion to table a motion: In parliamentary procedure, a motion to table a motion is a subsidiary motion that is made when a member seeks to postpone further discussion of the topic. This motion is often made when a member of the group feels that more and better information about a subject will be available in the near future and that it is not incumbent upon the group to make a decision immediately. This motion does not stop discussion, but rather postpones it to a later date. This motion cannot be used to interrupt a speaker and it requires a second. It is neither debatable nor amendable. It requires a simple majority for passage.

Motion to move the previous question: In parliamentary procedure, a motion to move the previous question is a subsidiary motion meant to conclude discussion on a particular topic. This motion is often made when a member of the group feels that the group has fully discussed a topic and is only repeating previously made arguments. If this motion is passed, the chairperson will then have the right to cease discussion on anything other than new points on the designated topic. This motion is neither debatable nor amendable. It cannot interrupt a speaker and it requires a second. It requires a two-thirds majority for passage.

Motion to limit or extend debate: In parliamentary procedure, a motion to limit or extend debate is a subsidiary motion whose purpose is to define how much time will be allowed for discussion of the topic. This motion is made when a group is under particular time constraints or when the members of the group feel that discussion has the potential to continue for an impractically long time. This motion may limit the number of speeches, may designate a time limit for each speech, or may limit the total amount of time to be spent in discussion. A speaker may not be interrupted with this motion. This motion requires a second and is both debatable and amendable. It requires a two-thirds majority for passage.

Motion to postpone to a definite time: In parliamentary procedure, a motion to postpone to a definite time is a subsidiary motion that is made when a speaker wants to table discussion until a designated point in the future. This motion is slightly different from the motion to table, in that it specifies when discussion will be resumed. It is typically made when a member feels the meeting has gone on too long or that discussion has become unprofitable at present. The motion to postpone to a definite time cannot interrupt a speaker and it requires a second. It is both debatable and amendable. It requires a simple majority for passage.

Motion to refer to a committee: In parliamentary procedure, a motion to refer to a committee is a subsidiary motion in which a special committee designated by the group is asked to study a particular problem and report back to the group at large at a later date. This motion often contains a recommendation as to who should be on the committee as well as the designated time at which the committee will report to the group. This motion is often made to prevent a regular meeting from running on too long. It may not be used to interrupt a speaker and it requires a second. It is both debatable and amendable. It requires a simple majority for passage.

Motion to amend: In parliamentary procedure, a motion to amend is a subsidiary motion made to alter a previously made motion. It may amend the previous motion in the following ways: adding more language; subtracting language; substituting language; or substituting an entirely new motion. Main, subsidiary, and privileged motions may all be amended. A motion to amend must be discussed and voted on immediately, before any other business is handled. These motions cannot be used to interrupt a speaker and they require a second. They are both debatable and amendable. They require a simple majority for passage.

Motion to postpone indefinitely: In parliamentary procedure, a motion to postpone indefinitely is a subsidiary motion made to prevent a vote on a pending main motion. If this motion is passed, discussion on the topic in question must cease for the rest of the current meeting. Also, the passage of a motion to postpone indefinitely suggests that most of the members of a group are not really interested in passing the main motion. A motion to postpone indefinitely cannot be used to interrupt a speaker and it requires a second. It is both debatable and amendable. It only requires a simple majority for passage.

Basics of Extemporaneous Speaking

In an extemporaneous speaking event, students select one of three questions and then prepare and deliver a speech within 30 minutes. During the 30-minute interval, students are given a selection of articles from magazines and newspapers. The extemporaneous speech is usually required to be approximately seven minutes long. It must be delivered without notes or other visual aids. Speakers are expected to deliver their message in a way that is informative to the audience as well as entertaining. Moreover, an extemporaneous speech must have a discernible structure; that is, an introduction, body, and conclusion.

Two Common Types of Extemporaneous Speaking Events

The two common types of extemporaneous speaking events are foreign extemporaneous speaking and domestic extemporaneous speaking. The only real difference between these two events is that foreign extemporaneous speaking takes foreign issues as its subject, whereas domestic extemporaneous speaking concentrates on issues particular to the United States. Both of these events have a similar format: Students are required to prepare and deliver a speech within a short amount of time, typically 30 minutes. Each round of competition contains between five and eight students. Judges rank the performances in order from first to last.

Structure of an Extemporaneous Speech

To be effective an extemporaneous speech must follow a discernible structure. At the beginning of the speech, the speaker will try to engage the attention of the audience with a memorable quotes or statistic. The speaker will then show how this interesting piece of data relates to his or her larger point. At this point, the speaker will fully introduce his or her topic. The speaker may need to define any words that may be unknown to the audience. After clarifying his or her thesis statement, the speaker will continue to substantiate this point with supporting arguments and evidence. Extemporaneous speaking competitions typically require the speaker to use a certain number of sources. In the conclusion of an extemporaneous speech, a speaker should make sure to restate his or her thesis and create a memorable or intriguing image or anecdote for the audience.

Basics of Original Oratory

Original oratory is probably the most popular event in a traditional high school forensic competition. In this event, each competitor is required to prepare and deliver a speech on a factual subject. Typically, the speeches are not allowed to be more than ten minutes long. The speeches delivered in an original oratory competition are often persuasive in nature. Each competitor is judged on the effectiveness of his or her speech, body control during delivery, the evidence marshaled on behalf of his or her argument, and the overall truth of his or her message.

Rules and Judges for an Original Oratory Competition

Original oratory competitions tend to abide by the same rules. First, orations are usually required to be between seven and ten minutes long. Each speaker has to memorize his or her oration and is not allowed to use note cards. Similarly, speakers are not allowed to use props or charts. Each oration may contain no more than 150 words or 30 seconds of quoted material; the rest must be original. The judges in an original oration contest are usually former competitors, speech and debate coaches, sponsors of the tournament, or parents. Family and friends of students are forbidden from judging.

Basic Structure of an Original Oration

Original orations tend to follow a basic structure. An oration will begin with an introduction in which the speaker attempts to engage the attention of the audience and introduce the main components of his or her message. Next, during the body of the oration, the speaker will attempt to show the audience why the subject is important to them. The speaker will need to maintain a balance between factual exposition and interesting detail; a good oration will simultaneously entertain and inform the audience. Finally, in the concluding section of the oration, the speaker will reiterate his or her main points and attempt to leave the audience with a lasting positive impression.

High School Policy Debate Competitions

High school policy debate competitions are a great opportunity for beginning debaters to get some experience in a tournament setting. It is typical for these debates to be held over two days. On the first day, the preliminary rounds of the policy debate competition are held. All of those students who qualify will participate in what are known as "out rounds" on the second day of the tournament. In these out rounds, debaters are judged against one another by a set of official judges, who eliminate one debater in each round. Eventually, the two best debaters will be pitted against one another in the final.

National Speech and Debate Tournament

Every year in early June, the National Forensic League hosts the National Speech and Debate Tournament. It is a weeklong tournament held in a different city every year. Only the best high school debaters are invited to compete in the national tournament; every year, only about 3,000 students participate. The tournament contains the following events: domestic extemporaneous speaking, duo interpretation, foreign extemporaneous speaking, humorous interpretation, dramatic interpretation, Lincoln-Douglas debate, original oratory, policy debate, public forum debate, and student congress.

National Forensic League

The National Forensic League administrates hundreds of high school competitive speech events. This group also coordinates changes to the rules of speech and debate competition. Every state has a subsidiary organization that pledges to abide by any rule changes made by the National Forensic League. Perhaps the most important function of the organization is to host the annual National Speech and Debate Tournament, which includes over 3,000 high school students. The NFL also publishes a monthly magazine, the Rostrum, on the subject of debate education. High school students who participate in speech and debate competitions are awarded points by the NFL.

General Objectives of a School Forensics Program

A school forensics program has a number of objectives. Perhaps most importantly, it aims to provide students with the opportunity to develop their public speaking and oral interpretation skills. To be effective, a school forensics program needs to offer frequent opportunities for all student members to practice these skills. Teachers should aim to develop in their students both verbal and nonverbal communication skills. They should also teach their students how to apply critical reasoning skills to the arguments and ideas of others. Students should learn how to organize their own ideas effectively. Finally, students should be able to dramatically interpret the literary works of others.

Social and Intellectual Benefits for Students Who Participate in a School Forensics Program

Students can expect to benefit in a number of ways from participation in a forensics program. By joining such a program, students develop their skills in oral and nonverbal communication and learn to effectively present an argument to a group. Forensics programs also give students the chance to develop strong research skills, which underlie the ability to construct a clear argument. Students will also build relationships among themselves and with students from other schools who participate in debate and speech competitions. Finally, for many students, participation in a forensics program is a springboard to other leadership opportunities.

Effect of Forensics Competition on School Relations

Perhaps the most overlooked benefit of school forensics programs is the strong relationships that develop among participating schools. During speech and debate competitions, students from various schools get to know one another through their shared interest in forensics. Many school teams travel overnight to participate in forensics competitions and through this experience are encouraged to make friends with people from different parts of the state and country. The National Forensics League is the umbrella organization under which all school forensics programs operate. This organization strives to cultivate relationships between schools through speech and debate.

Concepts of Oral Interpretation

Basics of Oral Interpretation

Although oral interpretation is a type of public speaking, it is very different than the delivery of a speech. For one thing, oral interpretation does not require the speaker to have written his or her own words. On the contrary, an oral interpretation presentation is a reformulation and expression of words written by someone else. In a sense, oral interpretation is a public and social form of storytelling. The work being interpreted may be a dramatic text, a work of prose, or a poem. Before the advent of radio and television communication, oral interpretation was the predominant form of information and entertainment. It is still very prevalent, although much more oral interpretation occurs through other media than in person.

Selecting a Text for Oral Interpretation

Perhaps the most important step in oral interpretation is selecting a proper text. Works of prose, poetry, and drama are acceptable texts for oral interpretation. It is important to choose a text that is appropriate for the audience. For instance, storytellers often take fairytales as their text, this is appropriate for an audience of children but may be too simplistic for an adult audience. Also, it is important to make sure the text is of an appropriate length given the time constraints. An effective oral interpretation may require significant dramatic pauses and periods of nonverbal communication. All of these features should be taken into account when determining whether a text is the right length.

Composite Recital

In the form of oral interpretation known as composite recital, two or more people will interpret various texts. All of the texts interpreted by the performers will have some common thread, whether it is author, theme, cultural background, or subject matter. Typically, an introductory speech precedes a composite recital. In this speech, the unifying thread will be presented and the various pieces to be interpreted will be introduced. In a typical composite recital, all of the performers will be grouped together on a stage and will take turns interpreting their material. Oral interpretation presentations usually require minimal set dressing.

Choral Speaking

In the form of oral interpretation known as choral speaking, a group of people joins their voices together to pronounce a single text. Perhaps the most famous example of choral speaking is the dramatic chorus in Greek drama. Only texts with a regular meter or rhythm can be used in choral speaking; other, more varying texts are too difficult to recite in unison. Different kinds of poetry have been incorporated into choral speaking with great results. Sometimes an individual speaker will deliver the verse and the group as a whole will deliver the chorus. In other cases, each individual will read a line and then the group as a whole will read the refrain.

Basics of Reader's Theatre

Reader's theatre is a form of group oral interpretation in which two or more individuals present a dramatic interpretation of a literary work. The presentation of reader's theatre is similar to that of a play, except the text is a work of prose or poetry rather than of drama. Also, reader's theatre typically has little set direction and scenery. Participants in reader's theatre often use elements of pantomime to suggest props. Because there are so few accessories in reader's theatre, the presenters tend to make exaggerated movements and display broad emotions. Reader's theatre is similar to the run-through performed by actors during the rehearsal of a play.

Dramatic texts in reader's theatre: On occasion, the participants in reader's theatre will use a work of drama rather than one of poetry or prose. Obviously, works of drama lend themselves to oral interpretation and therefore will require much less use of suggestion to indicate costumes and scenery. On the other hand, plays often have elaborate set directions, which may be beyond the scope of reader's theatre. When this is the case, the participants should either select another text or should include an introductory speech in which the potentially confusing aspects of the presentation are explained. In a more formal presentation, the participants may hand out a program that gives this information.

Folklore

Any story passed on by word of mouth until it becomes ingrained in a culture may come to be known as folklore. In other words, folklore is the set of narratives that circulate among the members of a community through oral interpretation rather than through writing. Various categories of folklore include legends, jokes, fairy tales, and fables. Even though people usually associate folklore with a bygone age, there is a great deal of modern folklore as well. Although most scholars declare that folklore must be fictitious, it is often based on themes and issues common to everyday "real life." For instance, there is a great deal of folklore surrounding the figure of Davy Crockett. Even though most of this folklore is exaggerated or untrue, it is based on events that actually happened to a real person. Many scholars concentrate solely on the characteristics of folklore in various cultures.

Folklore in Performance

Because it is an oral exercise, the creation and dissemination of folklore is by definition an act of performance. Folklore is traditionally allied with storytelling, though there are other ways in which it can be delivered. For instance, one of the most common forms of folklore at present is joke telling. Whenever someone tells a joke to a friend, he or she is engaged in a form of performance. This performance can be subjected to as much scrutiny and evaluation as a formal dramatic presentation. Indeed, all of the elements that define a successful performance (vocal control, nonverbal communication fluency, rapport with the audience) are essential to the delivery of folklore.

Storytelling

Storytelling is the craft of using words, gestures, and sounds to convey a narrative to an audience. At one time in human history, storytelling was the predominant form of information, entertainment, and self-knowledge for communities. Societies defined themselves based on the stories they told about themselves. By studying the stories that have been told in the past, scholars can gain insight into which qualities were particularly valued by a culture and the particular issues that caused the most anxiety for those people. Many people assume that storytelling is a dying art, though in fact it continues to thrive in various media. Television, movies, and radio, for instance, all use traditional elements of storytelling to develop powerful narratives.

Storytelling in Performance

Storytelling as a type of oral interpretation remains a popular form of entertainment even in this modern age of computers and televisions. Storytelling requires a narrative, which means it must have characters and a plot. Outside of these requirements, the storyteller has a great deal of creative freedom. Many storytellers incorporate sound effects and simple props into their performances. In any case, a speech communication instructor can assess a storytelling performance in the same way as he or she would any other oral interpretation. The success of the performance will depend on the fluency, preparation, and rhetorical skills of the storyteller.

Oral History

Oral history is any account of past events that is transmitted through the human voice rather than through writing. In the distant past, many cultures developed their self-identity primarily through oral history because they did not have the means to maintain a written history. At present, many historians focus on oral histories that are tape-recorded or videotaped. Many historians claim that oral history is a good way to give a voice to members of a society who, because of their marginal status, would otherwise not be able to make their voices heard. Also, oral history lends a human element to large, formerly impersonal historical events.

Oral History in Performance

Because it is a serious source of scholarly information, it sounds strange to speak of oral history as performance. However, in the broad sense of the word "performance," meaning any presentation involving speech and other forms of communication to an audience, it is clear that oral history fits the definition. Indeed, oral history is an important supplement to written history because information can be conveyed through the speaker's tone of voice and vocal mannerisms that cannot be expressed through printed language. Oral historians make a point of emphasizing those aspects of vocal performance that differentiate oral history from other forms of record-keeping.

Principles of a Text

Theme and Mood

To present an effective oral interpretation of a piece of literature, one must be able to discern the predominant theme and mood of the work. To discover the theme, one must read the text in its entirety and consider the general point the author is trying to get across. Even if the selection to be interpreted is only a portion of the entire work, one needs to understand how the selection fits into the work as a whole. This comprehensive reading should also reveal the mood of the piece. The mood is essentially the emotional content of the text. Naturally, the predominant mood of the text will have an enormous impact on the interpretation. Note that the mood of a text can change

Characterization

When interpreting a work of literature, one is often required to assume the point of view of a character in the text. To do this effectively, or to provide appropriate emotional emphasis in the portrayal of a given character, one needs to pay special attention to the author's use of characterization. Characterization is simply the way the author describes a character. Characterization may be direct, as in descriptions of the character's appearance and personality, or it may be indirect, in which character is revealed through actions or the ways in which other characters react to a given character. It is important not to take whatever a character says about himself or herself at face value because authors often create "unreliable narrators," or characters whose words are not necessarily to be trusted.

Structure

Structure is a combination of plot elements used to give shape and form to a text. These basically include beginning, middle, climax, and ending. With experience, a reader will develop a sense of the structure of a literary work. This sense of structure is invaluable when developing an oral interpretation. A sophisticated reader will be able to identify the climax, or most intense emotional point, in the text identifying the text's climax allows the reader to structure his or her interpretation to properly emphasize this peak dramatic moment. A reader should also be able to identify when an author is attempting to build tension in the text. The interpreter will want to convey this mounting emotion in his or her delivery.

Dialogue

If a selection for oral interpretation includes dialogue, the interpreter will have to make some important decisions about how he or she will handle this dialogue. For instance, the interpreter might decide to use different voices for the different characters in a conversation. Also, the interpreter will need to practice adjusting his or her voice to accurately represent the various moods of the characters involved in the dialogue. It is important for a speaker to understand these characters' motivations as well, as this information will allow him or her to produce a more sophisticated, nuanced interpretation of the words. Conversations have their own rhythms, frequently increasing and decreasing in tension. A good interpreter will be able to capture these rhythms in his or her presentation.

Diction

Diction is the unique style in which an author uses words and expressions. To interpret a work of literature effectively, one must understand both the denotative and the connotative meanings of the words an author uses. If necessary, the interpreter should look up all questionable words in the dictionary. Most importantly, the interpreter needs to understand how to properly pronounce each word. A dictionary will provide pronunciation guides as well as definitions. Besides understanding the pronunciation and definition of each word in the text, the interpreter also needs to know which words deserve special emphasis. Identifying key words in the text allows the interpreter to convey the appropriate meaning and correctly reflect the author's diction.

Punctuation

Although it is easy to pay little attention to it in a literary text, punctuation is an important element in oral interpretation. For instance, punctuation such as periods, colons, semi-colons, dashes, spaces, and spaces between sections of text all require pauses of varying duration. Also, when posing a question, it is typical to lift the voice to a higher register at the end of the sentence. Quotation marks in a sentence, of course, indicate that a character is speaking. In the case of such direct quotations, the interpreter will have to decide whether or not to use a different voice to represent each character who speaks.

Point of View in the Oral Interpretation of a Work of Prose

In the interpretation of a work of prose literature, it is especially important to have a sense of the point of view. The point of view is simply the perspective from which the story is told. For instance, in first person point of view, the story is told by one of the participants. First person perspective is distinguished by words like "I," "me," and "mine." When a story is told from the third person point of view, however, the narrator stands outside the story. Such a text is often told from an omniscient point of view, meaning the narrator knows everything, including the thoughts of all the characters. A limited omniscient point of view refers to a narrator who only knows certain information.

Treatment of Rhythm in the Oral Interpretation of Poetry

In the oral interpretation of poetry, one needs to be conscious of the rhythms and repetitions of the poem. Poetry is almost always written in a meter, or rhythm. Rhyming poetry will have what is known as a rhyme scheme, or a pattern of rhyming that occurs in the last word of each line. Also, many poems frequently repeat a single word, phrase, line, or set of lines. An interpreter needs to pay attention to these repetitions and vary his or her reading of the repeated words. The enunciation of the repeated words should evolve throughout the performance, so that the audience gets a sense of progress within the interpretation.

Technique of Emphasis in the Oral Interpretation of Poetry

In the oral interpretation of poetry, it is essential to recognize which words in a line deserve special emphasis. Too often, interpreters simply emphasize the last word in each line. Not only does this give their performance a repetitive and boring quality, it is also incorrect in cases where the line does not end with a comma, semi-colon, or period. When there is no punctuation at the end of a line of poetry, the interpreter should continue reading to the next line with no special emphasis. It is only through close study of the language and punctuation of a poem that an interpreter can learn the proper points of emphasis.

Oral Interpretation of Dramatic Works

Occasionally, a single individual will attempt the oral interpretation of a dramatic work. The obvious advantage of doing so is that the text has been designed for public performance, so the language and points of emphasis should be fairly clear. On the other hand, works of drama may call for elaborate staging and costumes beyond the scope of an individual oral interpretation. The interpreter will have to study the text to determine whether it can be adapted for oral interpretation. If too much action is called for in the stage directions, or if understanding the text depends on the presence of other characters, the interpreter would do well to look for another text.

Condensing Selections for Oral Interpretation

For a literary selection to be of an appropriate length for oral interpretation, it may be necessary to condense or cut the work. When editing a selection, it is important to leave all text that is essential to the meaning. For instance, when condensing a selection from a work of prose, it is a good idea to trim any references to characters or events that do not appear in the selection, unless these references have bearing on the meaning of the selection. The best rule of thumb is to always review the selection after the condensed version has been performed. If it still makes sense and conveys the same thematic meaning as the original, then the process of condensing the work can be considered successful.

Writing an Introduction to an Oral Interpretation Presentation

In some cases, an oral interpretation presentation will be preceded by a short introduction. If a selection is being taken from a larger work, or if a selection requires some context in order to be understood, it will be especially important to provide some guidance to the audience. There are a few key components to this kind of introduction. First, the presenter should outline the selection, including the major characters, back-story, and any other information necessary to understand the selection. A speaker also frequently explains why he or she has picked that particular selection and why it might be of interest to the audience. If the selection has any relevance to current events or to the lives of the audience members, this information would be meaningful to an introduction.

Necessity of Practicing for an Oral Interpretation Presentation

It may seem obvious, but it is absolutely essential to practice before an oral interpretation presentation. Practice begins with learning the text inside out, but it is not complete until the performance has been fully rehearsed several times. During these rehearsals, the performer should be timed to make sure his or her delivery does not exceed the time constraints. If possible, the performer should rehearse in front of an audience (perhaps of friends or other performers) so he or she can practice making good eye contact and directing his or her voice to the different parts of the room. Multiple rehearsals also give the performer a chance to experiment with different deliveries and gestures.

Analysis and Interpretation of Dramatic Presentations

During the preparation for a dramatic presentation, the director and the crew will need to analyze and interpret the text. The director must identify the central character, or protagonist, as well as the supporting characters and the main conflict in the text. The director should also identify the mood and theme of the play, as these factors will influence all of his or her other decisions, from casting and staging to vocal emphasis and lighting. The director should outline the general structure of the play in order to bring the action to its appropriate climax and resolution.

Analysis of Rhythm

One of the aspects of drama that receives less attention than it should is rhythm. Every play has a natural rhythm, or periods of intense action followed by lighter action. To avoid overtaxing the audience, a dramatist has to mix moments of high and low intensity. Typically, a play will have several small climaxes before reaching its most dramatic point, the major climatic scene toward the end of play. A period of resolution, known technically as the denouement, usually follows the climax. During the analysis of a play, the director and his or her staff should pay close attention to the rhythm of the text so they can bring that same rhythm into the dramatic presentation.

Analysis of Character

During the planning phase of a dramatic presentation, the director and his or her staff should pay close attention to the relationships between the various characters. Each actor should note the attitude of his or her character toward all the other characters in the play. In some cases, the relationships between even distantly-related characters will change subtly during a performance. The director needs to be able to point out these slight changes to the actors so they can be conveyed in the performance. Also, a dramatic performance will convey the unique relationships between characters, such as that of a father and son or brothers.

Benefits of Group Oral Interpretation

There are a number of advantages to performing group oral interpretation. First, it encourages more than one person to familiarize themselves with the text. Also, group members can motivate one another to higher achievement. Also, it is easier for a group to perform works having more than one character since it can be very difficult for one person to express all the different voices required by some texts. Group interpretation is also a good venue for people to gather and share their various ideas of interpretation and of literature. Finally, rehearsals tend to be more productive when there are other people present to critique one another's performances.

Use of Scripts in Choral Speaking

Typically, all of the participants in choral speaking use a script during the performance. Each participant should indicate on his or her script those lines that he or she will be required to speak. If there are any stage directions, these should be indicated on the script. It is a good idea to print the text in a double-spaced format and to number the lines so the cast can easily find their places. Additionally, the scripts should be distributed in advance of rehearsal so cast members can become familiar with where their lines occur throughout the script.

Motion and Position in Choral Speaking

For a choral speaking performance to be effective, the cast members need to practice speaking in unison. Only by beginning and ending each word at the same time can they achieve the clarity necessary to be understood. Also, if the cast is required to make any synchronized motions, these should be practiced as well. The intended effect will be successful only if the motion is performed precisely in unison. Finally, the director of a choral speaking group needs to organize the group by voice. Typically, any soloists will be positioned toward the front of the group. Those with deeper and stronger voices are usually placed in the back.

Memorization for an Actor

To be truly expressive, an actor needs to memorize his or her lines. This is in large part because the actor's concentration needs to move from the recitation of the mere words to the development of nonverbal communication methods and interpretation of character. If an actor is looking at cue cards or holding a copy of the script, he or she will not be able to gesture or move freely about the stage. Furthermore, he or she will not be able to make eye contact with the other actors or with the audience. It is most important to memorize lines before rehearsals begin in earnest. Even if an actor forgets some of his or her lines and requires a prompt during rehearsal, it is still better to start working without a script as soon as possible.

Motivation for an Actor

An actor's "motivation" does not mean his or her reason for participating in the play. Rather, it refers to the actor's identification of the motivations of the character he or she is playing. To effectively interpret a role, an actor needs to understand why the character behaves as he or she does. Without the right motivation, an actor will not be able to demonstrate effective emotion. Even the nonverbal aspects of a character's interpretation are dependent on the character's mood and motivation. Therefore, in order to transmit the right thematic message to the audience, the director and the actors need to have a good sense of each character's motivation.

Establishing Character Background for an Actor

Actors often talk about developing a character's background, or back-story. By this they mean establishing what the character's life and history were prior to the point at which the play begins. By understanding where a character is "coming from," an actor can gain insight into that character's motivation and emotional range. Sometimes this information can be discerned from the author's description of the character for instance, if a character is handicapped, it might be assumed that he or she has been in an accident in the past. Actors also get information from the character's dialogue and behavior. The director and actors need to collaborate to establish character background in order to accurately determine the characters' motivations.

Vocal Control

To effectively interpret his or her role, an actor must have excellent vocal control. An actor needs to be able to pronounce words clearly, so that every member of the audience will be able to understand the dialogue. In some cases, an actor may need to incorporate a regional dialect and have it be both credible and comprehensible. Some characters have particular vocal mannerisms, like a stammer or a lisp, which must be interpreted accurately. Finally, an actor must be able to convey the appropriate emotion with his or her voice at different times during a play. An actor who has a sense of his or her emotional vocal range can thereby save his or her most exaggerated vocal techniques for the climactic sections of the play.

Actor's vocal technique of projection: Actors often refer to the vocal quality of "projection, "by which they mean the level of force in volume with which words are delivered. To perform in front of a large audience, an actor needs to have enough projection so that everyone in the audience can hear and understand all the lines. Actors cultivate strong abdominal muscles and lungs so they can maintain their ability to project. Also, actors constantly work on combining clarity of expression with volume. A specific technique that actors use to increase the quality of projection is called "pointing." This is the technique of emphasizing particular words in a sentence, either by pausing before them or extending their enunciation. Pointing helps the actor's words to be understood.

How an Actor Handles Nonverbal Communication

An actor can handle nonverbal messages during a dramatic presentation in a number of different ways. It is important for the gestures to be appropriate, consistent, and tailored to the audience. Any nonverbal communication used must be appropriate to the character being portrayed; in other words, the gestures and vocal techniques need to be such that they seem right for the character. Also, a character's mannerisms must remain consistent from the beginning of the play to the end of the play. Finally, the ways in which an actor uses nonverbal communication must be expressive enough to be seen by everyone in the audience. When performing for a small audience, an actor can get away with more subtle nonverbal communication than he or she can when performing for a large audience.

How Movement Is Used in a Dramatic Presentation

There should be no random movements during a dramatic presentation. That is, all the positioning of the actors should be choreographed ahead of time. The entrances and exits of the characters are usually indicated in the text, but the proxemics may be at the discretion of the director. A sophisticated director can convey information about the characters and their interrelationships through their positioning onstage. At all times, however, the director needs to keep in mind the necessity of making the actors visible to the audience. Positioning should be one of the main focuses of rehearsal, and the director should experiment with different arrangements.

Basic Parts of the Dramatic Stage

A basic dramatic stage includes a single floor and an arch that extends from one side to the other. The section of the stage closest to the audience is referred to as downstage. The section of stage farthest away from the audience is known as upstage. When the stage directions call for movement to the right or left, this means from the perspective of the actors. Although most of the major set directions are included in a dramatic text, a director will have to come up with supplementary directions. These supplementary directions are known as "blocking."

Choosing an Appropriate Dramatic Script

When selecting a dramatic script for presentation, a producer needs to keep in mind the makeup of the audience. For instance, when a work is to be presented to a group of children, it should not deal with mature or violent themes. One of the best places to find a dramatic text is the local library. Most libraries have numerous anthologies containing famous plays. Once a play has been chosen, the producer needs to procure playbooks for all the members of the cast and crew. It may be necessary to pay royalties to the author or publisher of the play.

Process of Holding Auditions for a Dramatic Presentation

When holding auditions for a dramatic presentation, directors should have a basic idea of what type of actor they prefer for each role. At the same time, they should keep an open mind. Sometimes an actor will give a unique performance during the audition, thus changing a director's mind about what he or she needs for a given role. If an audition is "open," that means anyone is allowed to show up and try out. A "closed" audition means only invited actors are allowed to attend. If particular qualities or abilities are required of an actor to fill a given role, such as the ability to sing or play an instrument, these should be made known before the audition.

Typical Policy for Making Casting Decisions

When making casting decisions, directors adhere to a general policy. First, everyone who participates in an audition fills out a form with contact information. This audition form should also include space to indicate any conflicts of interest that might interfere with an actor's ability to appear in the dramatic presentation. During the audition itself, actors may read from a script or be asked to improvise. Sometimes actors will be instructed to prepare a short scene ahead of time. If an actor is going to be required to sing or dance during the presentation, these skills should be tested during the audition. Usually, a committee that includes the director and producers makes its casting decisions once all the auditions have been completed.

Feedback During Rehearsal

During rehearsal of a dramatic presentation, it is essential that the director and producers provide constant and specific feedback to the cast and crew. Rehearsals are a valuable opportunity for everyone involved in the performance to experiment with different techniques, so it is important for the director to let the actors and crew know what is working and what is not. In some cases, it may not be appropriate to give feedback immediately. To provide a venue for feedback, the director will set up regular meetings with each member of the cast and crew. By the time the dress rehearsal and first performance take place, the director should have already fully reviewed and approved the performances of the cast and crew.

Responsibilities of the Student Director and Stage Manager

A student director (also known as assistant director) helps make the director's job easier. He or she may transcribe notes dictated by the director during rehearsal, may help to implement the director's blocking plan, and may coordinate activities with the costuming, lighting, and sound departments. The stage manager has a number of practical responsibilities; including overseeing construction of the set and making sure that any set changes can be accomplished quickly. He or she is also responsible for organizing and managing the crew. A stage manager needs to be intimately familiar with the light and curtain cues in the play and must also have contingency plans in case things go wrong.

Responsibilities of the Business and House Managers

In a dramatic presentation, the business manager is responsible for overseeing all financial aspects of the performance. These include ticket sales, the cost of promotions, and the costs of production. In the case of professional presentations, the business manager also handles wages paid to cast and crew. The house manager, on the other hand, is responsible for handling the admittance and seating of the audience members. The house manager runs a crew of ushers, who help audience members find their seats. Ushers also clean up the auditorium after each performance. The house manager is responsible for maintaining the heat or air conditioning system in the auditorium as well.

Necessity of Makeup, Costumes, and Props

To be performed professionally, a dramatic presentation needs makeup, costume, props, and crews. Makeup is necessary to counterbalance the effects of bright stage lighting. The members of the makeup crew will need to practice applying makeup to each cast member before the first performance, so they can get a good idea of what makeup scheme is appropriate. Costumes are important for creating an air of verisimilitude in the performance. The costume crew acquires the necessary wardrobe and makes sure it fits the cast. The props crew is in charge of acquiring, caring for, and storing all the movable items used in a performance.

Interpersonal Communication Skills

Self-Concept

Self-concept is simply an individual's sense of himself or herself. Voluntarily or involuntarily, every person brings his or her self-concept to bear during interpersonal communication. Some of the aspects that make up a self-concept include personality, roles, aspirations, and past achievements. To a large degree, a person's self-concept is defined by his or her interactions with others, especially by their responses to what he or she says and does. Personality traits and other aspects of one's self-concept may become more pronounced if they are reinforced by the comments of others, since people often internalize the compliments and criticism they receive. Some individuals construct their self-concept in relation to someone they admire or despise. For instance, an individual might model himself or herself after some famous person and therefore evaluate his or her own words and deeds in comparison with those of that other person.

Low Self-Concept Can Be Changed Through Communication

Although it is a nebulous, complicated process, self-concept does change over time. One of the main factors that influences change in self-concept is interpersonal communication. Individuals largely determine their self-concept in relation to how they see others, and their views of others are primarily developed through communication. Although specific interactions—compliments and criticism in particular—can have a major impact on self-concept, it would be wrong to isolate a particular communication event as the sole determining factor in individual self-concept. The development and maintenance of self-concept is too complex and long-term to be traced back to one particular communication. Occasionally, interpersonal communications can cause an "identity crisis," or the radical questioning of one's self-concept. Even in its most extreme form, however, an identity crisis is simply a slight acceleration of the normal changes in self-concept.

Self-Concept Applies to Interpersonal Communication

During interpersonal communication, all the participating parties filter information through their own self-concept. Everyone naturally applies new information to their own self-concept. Often, however, self-interested concerns can make it difficult for a listener to get a true sense of what the other person is saying. As much as possible, listeners should strive to understand and take into account their own self-image, so they can be as objective as possible when evaluating an incoming message. Although a slight degree of egotism or self-centeredness is natural, these traits can hinder accurate and insightful listening. Therefore, the goal of speech communication education is to mitigate these distorting factors.

When two individuals have a conversation, their self-images and the images they hold of each other exert a great influence on the course of the conversation. For instance, imagine you are talking to your teacher. You have a self-image and an image of the teacher. You also have an image of how you hope your teacher sees you. Finally, you have an image of how you think your teacher actually sees you. Similarly, your teacher holds his or her own set of four images in mind. Obviously, then, even carrying on a simple conversation becomes a complicated event. Speech communication theorists assert that conversations tend to go better when there is less discrepancy between these various images. For instance, if your self-image is similar to the image you imagine your teacher has of you, you are less likely to have trouble coming up with appropriate things to say. Similarly, if your impression of what the teacher thinks of you is similar to what you hope the teacher would think of you, you are less likely to make outlandish claims or try to justify yourself.

Self-Disclosure

According to speech communication theorists, conversations work best when both parties are as honest and forthcoming about themselves as possible. In other words, when engaged in conversation, a person should strive to be as accurate as possible in revealing his or her self-image. This process is known as self-disclosure. To the degree that we hide information about ourselves, we prevent others from truly understanding us. There are a number of reasons why a person might not engage in total self-disclosure. Propriety, pride, and fear are probably the most common reasons for hiding information about oneself. Difficulty can also arise when one individual in a conversation has information about the other without the other party being aware of it. This kind of asymmetrical knowledge can create underlying but unexpressed tension in a conversation. Ideally, people should attempt to continually increase their level of self-disclosure while encouraging their interlocutor to do the same.

Low Self-Disclosure Can Be Supported

If we assume that self-disclosure is a positive value in conversation, we can then consider the ways in which it can be promoted. Obviously, it will not always be appropriate to simply demand that our interlocutor be entirely open and honest. Instead, the best way to encourage self-disclosure is to establish a comfortable, nonjudgmental environment for conversation. If a strong rapport and level of trust are established between the interlocutors, self-disclosure will follow naturally. When trying to promote self-disclosure in others, we should refrain from negative comments and harsh criticism. We should also remember to smile and be as warm as possible with our interlocutors, so they will become more comfortable about truly revealing themselves.

Alienation Can Influence Interpersonal Communication

If a supportive environment is the ideal state for self-disclosure, a state of alienation is the exact opposite. Alienation is a feeling of estrangement from other people. Alienated individuals view the world around them as cold and frightening, and they are therefore less likely to engage in self-disclosure. Many sociologists feel that the United States has an abnormally large number of alienated individuals. It should be noted that people with a long history of alienation will be especially unreceptive to efforts at honest and open communication. The natural response of someone who feels alienated is to retreat into him or herself and avoid exposure. For this reason, it is especially important to develop a supportive and welcoming environment, one that promotes self-disclosure. Over time, people who feel alienated can learn to trust others and experience the value of healthy self-disclosure.

Trust Can Improve Interpersonal Communication

For effective interpersonal communication to exist, the parties involved must trust one another. Note that trust does not necessarily connote affection. In fact, most people can think of others whom they do not particularly like but do trust. For the most part, the ability to trust develops in the early years of childhood and is based on the child's relationship with his or her parents. When parents honor the commitments they make to their children and take care of their responsibilities, those children ordinarily begin to develop trust in the correspondence between words and actions. Although it can be dangerous to be too trusting, interpersonal communication is generally improved when one has a natural trust of others, tempered by some measure of healthy skepticism. Furthermore, by becoming more trustworthy ourselves, we allow others to respond to our communications more openly and appropriately.

Selecting Criteria for the Evaluation of Interpersonal Communication

There are three steps in the evaluation of an interpersonal communication event: selecting the criteria for evaluation, describing the event, and making the evaluation. The first step, selecting the criteria for evaluation, establishes the qualities of communication that will be scrutinized. The particular criteria used to judge the quality of a communication event will vary depending on the kind of event. For instance, when evaluating a casual conversation, you might focus on warmth, clarity of expression, and comprehensibility. When evaluating a public speech, on the other hand, you might place more emphasis on audience analysis, appropriate gestures, and argument structure. In an informal setting, we would not expect a speaker to have his or her message rigidly organized. On the other hand, we would be surprised if a public speaker did not have a firm grasp and orderly delivery of his or her subject.

Describing an Interpersonal Communication Event

After selecting the criteria that will be used in the evaluation of an interpersonal communication event, one can turn to the task of describing the event itself. Naturally, the description of the communication event will emphasize those aspects, or channels, of the communication that correspond with the selected criteria. For instance, in the description of a public speech, one will naturally be more concerned with the structure of the speaker's argument and will therefore pay considerable attention to this subject when describing the event. When describing a casual conversation between friends, on the other hand, one might pay more attention to describing tone of voice and body language, as these communicate openness and ease. It is important for a description to mention all the communication channels the speaker uses.

Evaluating an Interpersonal Communication Event

After the criteria have been selected and the communication event has been described, one can set about evaluating the interpersonal communication event. This simply means using the information from the description to decide whether the speaker has done an adequate job of meeting the standards set by the selected criteria. For instance, if it has been determined that effective argument structure is an important criterion for a successful public speaker, it will be necessary to evaluate whether a particular speaker has met this criterion. The evaluation is important because it enables progress to be made in communication. In a way, the process of evaluating communication is similar to the response to feedback made by the speaker. Consciously or unconsciously, a speaker is constantly evaluating the effectiveness of his or her communication and making adjustments based on these observations.

Critics Function as Consumers of Communication Information

To be successful in interpersonal communication, one needs to become a conscious critic. This does not mean hunting out the flaws in other people, or emphasizing the negative aspects of communication events. On the contrary, being an effective critic means paying attention to both the strengths and weaknesses of a communication event. Whether we realize it or not, we are all, to a greater or lesser degree, critics of communication. For instance, from a young age we are all inundated with advertisements. Over time, we become less and less susceptible to advertising because we begin to identify and discount its communication strategy. We implicitly understand the intentions of the advertiser and are therefore skeptical of the message. Speech communication education seeks to expand this healthy skepticism into everyday interpersonal interactions.

Study of Nonverbal Communication

The study of nonverbal communication is divided into three categories: paralinguistics, kinesics, and proxemics.

Paralinguistics

Paralinguistics, a term that means "beyond language," emphasizes vocal productions and sounds not strictly considered language. So, paralinguistics includes all those noises a person can make to express meaning, as for instance grunts and snorts. In addition, paralinguistics includes elements of linguistic expression such as tone of voice, cadence, and pitch. A great deal can be communicated through the paralinguistic elements of speech. Indeed, the tone of a speaker's voice can either reinforce or contradict the words he or she is saying. Paralinguistics looks at the ways in which these elements contribute to communication.

Kinesics

Kinesics emphasizes the motions of the body that support and elaborate verbal communication. Gestures, facial expressions, and gesticulations are all considered in the field of kinesics. More generally, posture and overall body language are studied as part of kinesic observation. Note that the body motions of a speaker may either contribute to or detract from his or her message. For instance, an individual's facial expression may contradict what he or she is saying. As an example, consider an individual who is using strong language yet standing with his shoulders slumped and head down. Such an individual will be detracting from the confident message expressed by his language.

Proxemics

Proxemics focuses on the relative positions of the individuals who are taking part in a communication event. The dynamics of a communication event are different depending on the proximity and relative positions of the speaker and his or her audience. For instance, if a speaker is delivering his or her message from a raised platform, the effect is different than if he or she were casually strolling through the audience during the speech. Because of the subtle effects of positioning during a communication message, proxemics is frequently invoked by stage managers. For speech communication teachers, however, proxemic study will focus on unrehearsed and informal arrangements of people during communication.

Ways in Which Nonverbal Communication Patterns Are Learned

One of the main issues in nonverbal communication study is the degree to which nonverbal communication patterns are learned or inherited. Researchers are especially interested in whether or not particular gestures hold the same meanings throughout different cultures. In general, they have discovered that people learn basic nonverbal communication patterns from their parents and the other senior members of their community. At the same time, each individual develops his or her own idiosyncratic nonverbal mechanisms, which reinforce that individual's identity. Interestingly, people tend to use more individualized nonverbal communication techniques at moments of high excitement or stress.

Common Paralinguistic Factors

The three most important paralinguistic factors are pronunciation, articulation, and voice quality. Pronunciation is the ability to effectively make vocal sounds that achieve communication goals. Proper pronunciation is relative to an individual's culture. Articulation is the ability to make distinct sounds that are intelligible to another person. Voice quality is an individual's ability to pronounce the vowels and consonants that are common in a given language. For the most part, voice quality is directly tied to the pronunciation of vowels, since these sounds last longer and are therefore more responsible for an individual's characteristic sound. The collection of vowels and consonants that make up the tonal repertory of a culture are known as the set of phonemes.

Articulation of Consonants

Consonant sounds are created by stopping or redirecting a sound. For instance, an "s" sound is formed by pressing the tongue to the palette to slow down an escaping sound. Because consonants often depend on a percussive motion, it is possible to draw them out for a long time. Similarly, because of their short duration, consonants do not have as much effect as vowels on the quality of an individual's voice. Because consonants are articulated quickly, they are often more difficult to hear. For this reason, speakers need to be especially sure to clearly articulate them. When a conversation is heard at a great distance, often all that can be discerned is a long string of vowels sounds. Similarly, individuals who mumble are doing a poor job of articulating consonants. Many individuals focus on pronunciation, but clear articulation of consonants is a prerequisite for this skill.

Major Errors of Articulation

As a child learns a new language, he or she has a tendency to omit sounds from words. Over time, the child will include all of the sounds, but may not be able to effectively articulate some of the more difficult consonants. For instance, the "t" sound is one that is often omitted from words, as for instance in the contraction "don't," which is often pronounced as "don'." As an individual begins to speak more quickly, he or she is even more likely to omit these common consonant sounds. To a certain extent, these errors of articulation are not a problem. When they become chronic and extreme, however, they can make speech extremely difficult to understand.

Vocal Pitch

Vocal pitch is the measure of the frequency of a human voice. When the frequency is extremely high, we might say that a person has a whiny or nasal voice. When the frequency is extremely low, we might say that a person has a rumbling or deep voice. Individuals vary the pitch of their voices in order to emphasize or deemphasize certain words in a sentence. For instance, people often raise the pitch of their voices in the last word of a question. Speech communication instructors consider changes in pitch to be a form of nonverbal communication, since the changes in pitch do not themselves contain a linguistic message. Changes in pitch are often made during the pronunciation of a single vowel sound, or between syllables in a word. In some languages, as for instance Chinese, pitch variations actually communicate meaning and cannot be considered nonverbal communication.

Volume and Vocal Delivery

The volume of an individual's voice is simply the relative loudness or softness of it. The primary requirement of vocal volume is that it must be loud enough for the intended audience to hear it. As long as this requirement is met, a speaker can utilize varying levels of volume in order to emphasize or deemphasize words and phrases. Obviously, using a higher level of volume draws special attention to what is being said, whereas speaking softly tends to diminish the perceived importance of the message. In the employ of a trained and skilled speaker, however, changes in volume can be quite artful. For instance, a speaker who has fully engaged the attention of his or her audience may lower the volume in order to force the audience to listen closely.

Speed and Vocal Delivery

Speech communication instructors consider vocal speed to be a subdivision of paralinguistics. Vocal speed, or rate of speech, is simply a measure of how fast an individual articulates syllables. In most cultures, a rapid rate of speech indicates excitement or urgency, whereas a slow rate of speech suggests calm and thoughtfulness. However, some cultures have a naturally fast or slow rate of speech. For instance, Spanish is typically spoken quite rapidly, even when the speaker is communicating information that has a normal level of urgency. English, on the other hand, is a more slowly-spoken language, especially by the citizens of the United Kingdom. In part, these varying rates of speech are determined by the characteristics of the language. The fact that Spanish words tend to end in a vowel makes it easier to string them together rapidly.

Functions of Pauses in Vocal Delivery

Human speech is not just a constant stream of syllables. The placement and use of pauses during speech also plays an important role in forming meaning. The study of pauses in human speech is a subcategory of paralinguistics. A short pause is often used to denote the end of a sentence or clause. In many ways, short pauses are used like commas. Long pauses, on the other hand, are more similar to periods or the ends of paragraphs. When a speaker takes a long pause, he or she may be allowing what has been said to sink into the minds of the audience. Individuals often pause as they search for the right word. Other times, individuals will insert a slight pause into a sentence to create a level of suspense before the thought is finished.

Nonverbal Communication

Enhance Spoken Words

Nonverbal communication is the ability to enhance or elaborate on the words of the speaker. In particular, hand gestures and changes in vocal rhythm and volume have the ability to add expressiveness to what is being said. Many times, the gestures and vocal mechanisms of the speaker simply emphasize his or her message; at other times, however, the speaker may detract from or undermine his or her message with contradictory gestures. Hand gestures and gesticulations have the ability to dramatize a communication event. By giving the audience things other than words to concentrate on, the speaker engages and entertains them.

Feedback

Although nonverbal communication is typically thought of as supplementary to the words being spoken during a communication event, it can also serve a vital purpose as feedback. The gestures, eye movements, facial expressions, and posture of the audience often indicates their level of engagement more accurately and honestly than verbal criticism. It is very difficult to hide extreme boredom or rapt attention. The nonverbal communication of the audience will indicate their level of interest and acceptance of the message of the speaker. The speaker can then adjust his or her message accordingly.

Alter the Meaning of Spoken Words

At times, the nonverbal communication produced by a speaker will give a slightly different message than that of the speaker's words. This is often the case when a speaker is attempting to introduce an element of irony into his or her message. For instance, if at the conclusion of a bad movie one friend says to another, "Well, that was a good use of my time," but smiles while saying the words, the other friend might assume that the message is being delivered with sarcasm. In other words, the speaker does not literally mean that the movie was a good use of time, but rather wishes to indicate that it was a waste of time. A message is being delivered, but the nonverbal communication accompanying the words creates a complex message different than the mere words being spoken.

Can Create Contradictory Communications

Sometimes, a speaker's nonverbal communication is contradictory to the words he or she is speaking. This can often create confusion and conflict. For instance, imagine a person is in distress. In some cultures, it is not considered dignified to ask another person for help, even in emergency situations. So a person in dire need of assistance might be saying he or she does not need help, even though observation of nonverbal signs says otherwise. Obviously, this will create conflict in the mind of the audience, who will want to obey the wishes of the person but will also want to lend assistance to a person in need. When an individual directly contradicts his or her words with his or her nonverbal communication, it becomes much more difficult for the communication message to be interpreted.

Four Proxemic Distances

Speech communication theorists distinguish four essential proxemic distances: intimate distance, personal distance, social distance, and public distance. Intimate distance is the degree of separation common to individuals who know each other very well and are comfortable being physically intimate, for instance parents and children or mates. Intimate distance is at most 2 feet. Personal distance, meanwhile, is around 2-1/2 feet. It is the distance maintained between two individuals who know each other and are engaged in a friendly, casual conversation. Social distance, usually defined as being from 4 to 7 feet, is the appropriate distance for impersonal and formal conversations. Public distance is 12 feet or more and is the amount of distance appropriate for the delivery of speeches to a group of people. Public distance is great enough to focus the attention of the audience on an individual speaker.

Emphasis on Geographic Relationships in Proxemics

In their study of proxemics, speech communication theorists place a great degree of emphasis on geographic location—that is, the relative positions of the participants in a communication event. To begin with, the distances between the various parties are important; the closer the participants in a communication event, the more intimate with one another they can be assumed to be. If one individual is placed above the other members of the communication event, he or she can be assumed to have some sort of elevated status or authority. When individuals are placed around a round table, on the other hand, we may assume that they are equal in importance, and that a democratic discussion rather than a lecture will take place.

Proxemics Can Define Boundaries

The proxemics of a communication event often indicates the boundaries of the parties involved. Individuals have a concept of personal space and territoriality, and tend to be defensive if they believe another person is encroaching on their area. A teacher who lectures from a podium at the front of the class, for instance, would be made uncomfortable if a student got out of his or her chair and stood next to the podium. Similarly, an informal conversation might become uncomfortable for one of the parties if there is too little distance between him and the other participants. For the most part, the appropriate distances between people during a communication event are indicated without explicit mention. In part, the appropriate distance is a cultural designation. However, participants in a communication event can indicate their preferred position through gestures, or simply by moving forward or back.

Proxemics Can Define a Communication Event

The relative positions and distances between the participants in a communication event can indicate a great deal about the quality of the event, even when none of the content of the message is known. For instance, when two people are standing very close to one another during a conversation, we can assume that they are intimate with one another and are discussing a subject of personal interest to each. On the other hand, if two individuals are standing at a considerable distance from one another and avoiding eye contact, we can assume that they either do not know each other very well or they are not well disposed to one another. If one party attempts to close the distance with the other party and the other party resists, we can assume that the first party desires a greater degree of intimacy than does the second.

Proxemics Can Define Interpersonal Relationships

The evolution of interpersonal relationships can be charted by the changes in proxemics. When two people first meet, they are likely to maintain a social distance, between 4 and 7 feet. This distance indicates formality and impersonality. If the two people develop a closer relationship, however, they will likely begin to stand closer to one another during communication. Another scenario in which proxemics denotes interpersonal relationship is when the parties have varying degrees of power. For instance, communication events in which one person is positioned by himself or herself while the others are facing him or her indicate that the isolated individual has a greater degree of power than the others.

Importance of Listening

For most students, the vast majority of information is obtained through listening. Despite the large amount of reading that most students have to do, they still take in more information through their ears than through their eyes. Good listening is an essential part of the communication process because it advances the interests of both the speaker and the listener. Obviously, the listener needs to understand and remember what he or she hears in order to consider the information accurately. At the same time, the listener protects his or her own interests by developing an accurate impression of what the other person has to say. Meanwhile, the ability of the speaker to have his or her message be effective depends on the listening skills of the audience.

Listening for Comprehension

Although listening appears to be a passive process, it must be active in order to be effective. Indeed, the listener should have a purpose for listening. The precise purpose of listening need not be conscious in the mind of the listener. Speech communication teachers generally distinguish four intentions of listening: comprehension, criticism, empathy, and appreciation. These intentions are often intermingled in the same act of listening. When we listen for comprehension, we are trying to understand the message the speaker is communicating. In order to listen for comprehension, we need to know the standards of grammar and punctuation in English as well as the common forms of argument. We also need to have an understanding of the context in which the words are spoken so we can understand the relationship between message and context.

Listening for the Purposes of Criticism

Most speech communication teachers will say that in order to listen for the purposes of criticism, one must also be listening for comprehension. It is true that to accurately assess the quality of a verbal communication, one must understand the content of the communication first. To a certain degree, however, we all apply critical listening skills to communication we have yet to fully understand. For instance, when we hear an advertisement on the radio, we know immediately that the speaker is trying to sell us something, which makes us naturally receptive or skeptical of the message, depending on our preexisting interest in the product or service. In such a case, our critical listening skills are influencing our listening even before we have begun to comprehend the content.

Listening for Empathy

People often listen to one another as a demonstration of empathy. Empathy is the ability to understand and appreciate what another person is going through despite not having the same experience oneself. One of the ways a person can express understanding and compassion for others is simply by listening to them. Listening to someone indicates that his or her problems are worth your time. Most people find that not only is listening a good way to demonstrate empathy, but it is also a good way to develop empathy. It seems that when we listen to one another, we gradually develop a sense of each other's internal worlds, and we come to treat each other with more compassion.

Listening for Appreciation

In many cases, people listen not necessarily for information but simply to appreciate the quality of what another person is saying. Many conversations are designed for the entertainment of the listener so it is not absurd to say that one listens to another person talk with the same appreciation one would have when listening to a piece of music. At the same time, it is important to take the speaker seriously on his or her own terms. If the speaker is trying to be gravely serious, it may not be polite to simply listen for appreciation. In many cases, though, and especially when listening to a speaker who is exceptionally fluent or more interesting, it is appropriate for a listener simply to appreciate the sounds and meaning the speaker is conveying.

Physical, Mental, and Emotional Obstacles to Listening

A number of things can prevent a person from listening effectively. Perhaps the most common is an external distraction, like background noise or confusing motion. A listener may also be experiencing internal distractions, however, such as anxiety or other preoccupations. Many people are desperate to express themselves and fail to listen to other people because they are so focused on what they themselves want to say. Also, many people have personal biases regarding what the other person is saying that prevent them from listening effectively. Any of these problems can prevent effective interpersonal communication.

Listening for Content in Interpersonal Communication

In almost every listening situation, the audience is required to listen for information. A communication can only be considered effective if the message communicates the information intended by the speaker. The feedback from the audience indicates the degree to which the information has been received accurately. When the audience is required to ask for clarification or repetition of the message, it is possible that the speaker has been ineffective in delivering his or her information. Moreover, if the audience provides no verbal feedback about a delivered message, it is possible that they either did not understand any of the message or are simply not interested in the message. Of course, when there is no verbal feedback it is also possible that the audience simply understood the transmitted message perfectly and they require no clarification or elaboration.

Problems Created by Unwillingness to Listen

Communication can be significantly obstructed when the intended receiver is unwilling to listen. This is a common situation on television talk shows, when all the guests and the host try to talk at once. When this occurs, no one is listening and therefore no messages can be considered complete. In order for a communication events take place, all the parties involved must accept that there can only be one speaker at a time. Frequently, the unwillingness to be a receiver is a symptom of a poor interpersonal relationship. Unwillingness to listen is a classic sign of disrespect. Sometimes, however, a failure to listen is simply the product of unfamiliarity between two parties. With a little patience and practice, this obstacle can be overcome and complete communication events can take place.

Interpersonal Communication

For a communication event between two people to be effective, both parties need to alternate the roles of speaker and receiver. Moreover, each receiver should ensure that the message of the speaker is fully understood before delivering his or her own message. Through the use of feedback, such as clarifying questions and comments, the speaker's message can be elaborated and made plain. A conversation cannot really move forward until both parties understand what has been said. This is not to say that the two parties are required to agree on what has been said. On the contrary, some of the best conversations are those in which two parties calmly and descriptively elaborate their differences. To be effective communicators, people need to be able to play the roles of both the speaker and the receiver with skill and dexterity.

Nonverbal feedback in interpersonal communication: To be an effective receiver of communication, a person must be able to give clear nonverbal feedback. In particular, facial expressions are a key way of signaling interest and understanding— or the lack thereof. If a person can display subtle gradations in understanding and interest with his or her face, he or she is much more likely to receive a refined and well-adjusted message. Traditionally, smiles and head nods are good indications that the message is being understood, and that the listener agrees. On the other hand, a shake of the head or a frown tends to indicate disagreement with the speaker's message or, sometimes, an inability to comprehend the content. What many people forget is that the receiver in a communication event must be as active and engaged as the speaker for the event to be considered a success.

Verbal feedback in interpersonal communication: To be an effective receiver, a person needs to be able to issue timely and thoughtful verbal feedback. For instance, a receiver needs to be able to ask pertinent questions if he or she does not understand a particular aspect of the delivered message. At the same time, the receiver needs to be able to describe his or her reaction to the delivered message, whether it be confusion, agreement, or disagreement. Questioning that encourages the speaker to elaborate and refine his or her message often leads to new insights not contained in the original message. In pedagogy, this is known as the Socratic Method. In terms of verbal feedback, however, a receiver's most important function is to continually indicate his or her level of understanding of the delivered message.

Process of Creative Listening

Speech communication instructors often use the phrase "creative listening" to describe extremely engaged receivers who are constantly encouraging the speaker to develop and specialize his or her message. An extremely good listener can often discern implications and ideas inherent in the message that may not have been known even to the speaker. In this way, a creative listener can actually add value to the content of the message. Some of the best conversations involve interplay between speaker and creative listener, as each plays ideas off the other until new and exciting conclusions are reached. Creative listening also demonstrates the receiver's interest and respect for the speaker. Often, this has the effect of encouraging the speaker to improve and expand his or her message.

Psychological Effects of Listening

Simply listening to another person can have profound psychological implications. Indeed, the entire field of psychoanalysis is largely based on the idea that having a sympathetic audience for one's problems is profoundly therapeutic. Many people pay a great deal of money simply to have a sympathetic listener who can offer some professional advice. Psychoanalysts are especially skilled at creative listening. That is, they are able to "unpack" the message of the speaker and discern new, possibly hidden meanings. Numerous studies have indicated that the process of verbally elaborating and describing personal issues eases the burden of stress on the mind, regardless of whether the interpretation of these issues is accurate or constructive.

Relationship Between Defensiveness and Good Listening

Defensiveness can be extremely limiting to an individual's ability to listen properly. When a person is defensive, he or she is overly concerned with protecting his or her own interests. Defensiveness is especially prevalent in interpersonal communications in which the two parties do not trust one another. However, some paranoid individuals may be naturally more inclined to defensiveness than others. The problem with defensiveness is that it indicates that the attention of the listener is on his or her own concerns, rather than on the content of the message being delivered. To the degree that a listener is not focusing on the message being delivered, his or her ability to understand and respond to the message will be impaired.

Various ways that defensiveness can impair communication: Speech communication theorists identify a number of ways in which defensiveness can impair effective and accurate communication. These ways are basically defined by the attitude of the listener. For instance, some defensive listeners adopt an overly evaluative posture, in which they indicate that it is up to them to decide whether the speaker is competent or not. Other defensive listeners adopt a self-consciously apathetic attitude, as if to indicate that they are above being interested in the message of the speaker. Another common listening attitude for a defensive individual is certainty, or the assumption that he or she already knows the content of the message. This attitude draws the speaker up short and makes it difficult for him or her to continue communicating.

Active Listening

Active listening is a technique of communication reception in which the listener tries to develop an empathic relationship with the speaker. Proponents of this form of listening declare that a great deal of listening contains an unhelpful evaluative aspect, to the extent that the speaker continually feels in danger of being criticized by the listener. In active listening, on the other hand, the listener makes an effort to fully experience the thought process of the speaker before even beginning to judge. Perhaps most importantly, active listening is a skill that is developed over time. To fully engage with what someone is saying, the listener must practice subverting his or her own ego and focus instead on the perceived interests of the speaker.

Cultural Demographics

One way of looking at culture is through the lens of category distinctions. The process of dividing people into categories is commonly known as demographics. The most common demographics are age, gender, sexual orientation, religious affiliation, ethnicity, and socioeconomic status. When an individual considers his or her own culture, he or she typically considers it as a set of memberships in these various categories. Those who study and teach speech communication are constantly considering the prejudices and values that influence speech and the interpretation of the spoken word. Part of the process of speech communication instruction is to bring the implicit cultural information in speech to light so that it can be analyzed and critiqued.

Identification with Demographic Categories

In speech communication, one is required to view speech through the lens of received and lived culture. In other words, one is required to consider how elements of culture influence the medium and message of speech, as well as the interpretation of the spoken word. One of the most important aspects of an individual, then, will be the extent to which he or she identifies with various demographic categories. Some people, for instance, have a strong identification with their ethnic or religious background, whereas others base their self-concept more on their gender or age. Age, of course, is a demographic identification that changes with time. Indeed, all demographic identifications may change with time, as an individual acquires more information and critically evaluates the prejudices and values of his or her culture.

Cultural Ideology

Whether consciously or not, every individual has adopted certain ideas, patterns of thought, and prejudices from his or her native culture. This native worldview is known as a cultural ideology. The cultural ideology of a particular group permeates every aspect of the group's existence. It defines what is important in the group, what is right or wrong in the group, and how members of the group should behave. The aspects of an individual's native ideology are often so ingrained that they are considered "common sense" and never really held up to scrutiny. Ideologies are important because they provide individuals with a moral compass and a sense of pattern in the world; however, it is important to develop an ability to think clearly and objectively about one's own ideology.

Cultural Hegemony

Cultural hegemony is any relationship in which one party is dominant and one party is submissive and in which both roles are agreed upon by the participants. Every culture establishes basic hegemonies, in part as a way of organizing the populace. For instance, in Asian cultures it is typical for the husband to impose his will on the wife, although she may subtly exercise power in her own right. Both partners agree that this is the proper hegemonic relationship between married couples. The hegemonies are not necessarily bad; in fact, they are useful ways of distributing power and responsibility in a society. However, students of speech communication need to be conscious of the ways in which language establishes and reinforces hegemony. Over time, it may be necessary for a culture to modify its hegemonies in response to the repressed needs of certain people.

Cultural Enactment

Cultural enactment is the process in which an individual fulfills with his or her words or behavior the expectations of his or her culture. In other words, cultural enactment is the "acting out" of cultural values. All of us are engaged in cultural enactment throughout our lives. When we get up in the morning, go off to work, and fulfill our roles as professionals, we are adhering to the expectations of our society. When we relate in a certain way to our family members, we are fulfilling our roles as mothers, fathers, brothers, sisters, etc. In speech communication, we study cultural enactment as it is performed in language. Whether consciously or not, we are constantly adhering to the expectations of society with our manner of speaking and with the message we present. Speech communication seeks to analyze this process.

Cultural Embodiment

Although every person grows up and develops with a particular cultural background, very rarely do we take the time to objectively consider it. In part, this is because it is very difficult to put into words the ideology that supports our worldview. Nevertheless, through our speech we are constantly producing and reinforcing the values shared by the members of our community. This process of expressing cultural assumptions is known as cultural embodiment. In literal terms, "cultural embodiment" means giving a body to the unconscious values and beliefs held by a particular culture. In speech communication studies, we are particularly interested in cultural embodiment through language. One of the goals of studying speech communication is to acquire an objective understanding of one's own culture as it is reflected in speech.

Demographic Analysis

Before delivering a speech, a speaker should, if possible, engage in some basic demographic analysis. The following are the most important demographic categories: age, education, gender, group membership, and cultural background. In many groups, all the audience members will be of the same general age, and the speech can therefore be tailored to their maturity level. As far as education, it is important to know about the audience's experiences and knowledge regarding the topic before the speech begins. Many times, the members of the audience will all belong to a specific group, such as a school class or a civic organization. Finally, the cultural background of a group should be considered because the group's values, taboos, predilections, and ethics could be offended by the speech.

Nonverbal Communication

Nonverbal communication is the set of ways in which humans send and receive messages without using words. For teachers, it is just as important to be effective nonverbal communicators as verbal communicators. They are essential aspects of the teaching process and can sometimes even be more effective than a verbal reminder. Nonverbal communication includes gestures, facial expressions, proximity, humor, posture, body orientation or touching. Being aware of the ways the students communicate nonverbally can also assist teachers in getting messages about how their students are learning. Sometimes sending signals can reinforce learning more effectively, because they are implicit and students will learn how to react to your nonverbal communication more readily because it tends to be less confrontational than direct statements.

Group Communication

Purpose of a Discussion Group

One special form of interpersonal communication is the discussion group in which a small number of people gather together for a particular purpose. The purpose may be to solve a problem, to organize a collective effort, or simply to elaborate and analyze a controversial issue. Sometimes, discussion groups are held in a ritual fashion, as for instance in the case of book clubs or Bible study groups. Speech communication theorists assert that regular and organized discussion groups typically have better communication. Also, discussion groups seem to function better when there is a clear and explicit hierarchy among the members, whether there is one leader of the discussion or none at all.

Characteristics of a Positive Discussion Group

For a discussion group to function effectively, a good sense of rapport and understanding must exist among the members of the group. These positive sentiments are more easily cultivated in groups that meet regularly. For new groups, establishing a positive environment for discussion is the responsibility of the chairperson, leader, or moderator. Unless a comfortable discussion environment is established, it will be difficult for the group to accomplish its goals. Time and again, research studies suggest that relationships between people have far-reaching effects on the progress and ultimate success of organizations both great and small. Discussion groups are no exception to this tendency.

Importance of Morale and Efficiency for a Discussion Group

For a discussion group to be effective, the group needs to have a high sense of morale. Morale is a general expression used to describe the attitude of the members of the group in regard to the activities of the group. If the members of the group enjoy one another's company and feel like the group meetings are worthwhile, morale will be high. Morale is also linked to situations in which the members of the group know their respective roles. When everyone knows his or her job and responsibilities, there is much less resentment and blaming for unaccomplished work. Similarly, the degree to which a discussion group is productive in pursuit of its goals will determine the effectiveness of the group. If, after several meetings, the members of the discussion group observe that progress is being made toward long-term goals, they will be more likely to commit themselves to the group and make any necessary changes to promote its effectiveness.

Importance of Togetherness for a Discussion Group

Research into discussion groups suggests that a sense of togetherness is essential for the promotion of discussion group goals. When the members of the group feel tied to one another, they are more likely to go out of their way to help one another and promote the progress of the group. In other words, the members of a cohesive group subvert their own goals in the interest of promoting the group goals. Also, the members of a cohesive group are more likely to communicate any personal problems that may affect the progress of the group. Communication becomes highly efficient and constructive criticism does not derail group activities. Cohesiveness can be built by creating an atmosphere in which the group members take an interest in one another and are respectful of each other's feelings.

Building a Positive Social Environment for a Discussion Group

Discussion group leaders can actively promote a positive social environment in a number of different ways. One easy thing to do is to allow the members of a group to get to know each other during the first group meeting. Many group leaders begin with a few "icebreaking" activities, in which the members of a group share a little bit of information about their personal lives and therefore become more comfortable. It is especially useful to have all the members of a discussion group describe what they are hoping to get out of the group work, as this establishes a climate in which all group members are openly working toward communal goals. It is natural for the members of a new group to feel a bit apprehensive during the first meeting. As much as possible, the group leader should seek to mitigate this apprehension by promoting warmth and positivity.

The Relationship Between Disagreement and Cohesiveness in a Discussion Group

It may seem like a paradox, but groups with a high level of cohesiveness tend to have a higher incidence of disagreement. The simple reason for this is that in a cohesive group the members feel comfortable enough with one another to disagree. In other words, the group members do not worry that a disagreement will destroy the group. Also, a cohesive group has likely established positive channels for constructive disagreement, so members are assured that conflicting opinions will not be viewed harshly by the other group members. Furthermore, cohesive groups often discover that frequent disagreement can be a stimulus to improve effectiveness in group discussion. When all the group members agree with one another, they do not raise pertinent objections and do not subject ideas to enough scrutiny.

Establishing Roles in a Discussion Group

For a group discussion to be effective, it is important that the group members have established roles. Speech communication research suggests that even if roles are not made explicit at the beginning of the discussion, after an hour or so individuals will naturally assume specialized roles. For instance, once the discussion gets rolling, it is natural for one or two leaders to emerge. Similarly, a discussion usually has two or three individuals who do not advance the discussion necessarily, but offer insightful critiques of what has been said by others. The formation of an individual's role within a group is a constantly evolving process in which the individual's personal desires and thoughts are combined with the needs and reactions of the group.

Basic Principles of Role Emergence

The emergence of individual roles in a group discussion is the result of interplay between the individual and the group. In other words, an individual is not solely responsible for his or her role, and neither is the group solely responsible for designating that individual. Once the members of the group have assumed tentative roles, the other members of the group assess the value of each role. That is, a hierarchy begins to develop within the group. Those individuals who have emerged as the leaders of the group are given a higher status. Group members look to them for direction, their opinions carry more weight, and the other group members tend to listen to them more closely. Lower status group members, on the other hand, may feel that their opinions are not valued and that they are not really being given the full attention of the group. Over time, however, group roles can shift, and individuals can gain or lose status.

Characteristics of a Leader

Perhaps the most important role within a discussion group is the leader. Research suggests that most people, given the option, would prefer to be the leader. Indeed, most people lead in at least one area of their lives, whether at school, at home, or at work. However, some people have a natural gift for leadership. In a discussion group, these individuals tend to speak more, be more forthright with their opinions, and project more confidence with their nonverbal communication. Of course, individuals can also develop leadership traits over time. Some people do not really blossom as leaders until they reach adulthood. Although our society values democracy, it seems clear that discussion groups function most effectively when there is some form of leadership. Perhaps the essential point is that, to be effective, leadership must be a designation agreed upon by all members of the group.

Characteristics of a Central Person in a Discussion Group

Speech communication instructors often refer to a "central person" in a discussion group. A central person is one who has such a strong personality that he or she cannot help but influence the group. A central person may have a positive or negative effect on the group. Central people are often funny, charming, and charismatic. However, their charisma may distract the attention of the group from its intended goals. Speech communication instructors are interested in central people because of their random and destabilizing effects on groups. At times, the presence of an influential central person can lead a group to high achievement; at other times, the manipulations and distractions of the central person can negatively affect the group.

Effects of Changing Membership on a Discussion Group

The effect of membership changes within a discussion group is destabilizing. When new members are added to a group, they must quickly assume roles in order to avoid obstructing the current progression of group work. If a group member is removed, on the other hand, the remaining members must try to fill the void by assuming different responsibilities. In general, it seems that when the members of a group change, the roles of every other group member are affected to a greater or lesser degree. Afterward, a brief period of instability ensues, in which the group is less effective than before. It is important for discussion groups to recognize the inevitability of this down period, and to be patient as roles are reestablished.

Basic Principles of Formal Leadership

Sometimes the roles in a discussion group are determined ahead of time. Speech communication instructors refer to this kind of group as having a formal organization. A formal organization will almost always have a designated leader. Furthermore, the other members of the group will probably have their relative status designated over time, as well. Unlike a free-form group, in which roles emerge and evolve over time, a formal discussion group features static group roles. At times, this can create inefficiencies in the group, as for instance when the designated leader is ineffective at discharging his or her duties. Similarly, group members with lower status may gradually develop skills that would otherwise lead to an increase in the importance of their role. The rigid nature of a formal hierarchy, then, can inhibit discussion if it is not managed properly.

Characteristics of Group Discussion

When speech communication instructors use the phrase "group discussion," they are referring to a single meeting or group of meetings of a small number of people who have a similar, agreed-upon set of goals. The minimum number of people required for a small group discussion is three, and whereas the maximum number is not set in stone, it is generally agreed that a group of more than fifteen will have a hard time managing a democratic discussion. Ideally, a small group discussion will have about five members. This seems to be the maximum number of people who can participate fully in a discussion. When a group has more than five members, it is common for the extra members to remain silent for the most part.

Characteristics of an Isolated, One-Time Meeting

In some cases, a small group discussion meeting will be held only one time. The dynamics of this kind of meeting are slightly different than those of a set of meetings held regularly over a period of time. For instance, a one-time meeting does not provide enough time for roles to develop and emerge, so it is beneficial if a group organization is established beforehand. As much as possible, the members of the group should become familiar with one another rapidly so the business of the discussion can begin without delay. Effective leadership is especially important when administrating a one-time meeting, as there will be no time to waste on role development and making acquaintances.

Characteristics of an Ad Hoc Meeting

Small group discussions are sometimes organized to address a particular problem. Speech communication instructors refer to these meetings as ad hoc groups, from the Latin phrase meaning "for a particular purpose." An ad hoc group may meet only once or it may meet several times until the intentions of the group have been realized. It is likely that the members of an ad hoc group will not have met each other before the first group meeting. However, unlike the members of the one-time meeting, the members of an ad hoc meeting group can assume they will be in contact with one another until their mission is complete. This tends to encourage a bit more solidarity. Also, an ad hoc discussion group provides more opportunity for role emergence and development.

Role of a Chairperson in Leading an Isolated Meeting

A discussion group that meets only once requires effective leadership more than any other kind of group. To swiftly and effectively lead a one-time discussion group, a chairperson must establish ahead of time the precise purpose of the meeting. This purpose should be known to all group participants. The discussion should be structured to achieve the goal and, as much as possible, environmental distractions should be minimized. Any preparatory materials required for the discussion should be procured ahead of time. It is also important to determine the necessary outcomes of the meeting the chairperson needs to know what sort of information constitutes a conclusive decision by the discussion group. He or she needs to know what details have to be decided upon before the group can adjourn. Finally, the chairperson needs to know and explain the mechanisms for putting into place the decisions made during the discussion.

Structure for leading a one-time meeting: Although every one-time meeting will be slightly different, depending on the structure, membership, and intentions of the meeting, there is a basic structure a chairperson can follow. First, the chairperson should call the meeting to order and announce the intentions of the discussion. The chairperson should then lead the discussion, heading off any digressions and maintaining the group's focus on its overall goals. After a sufficient amount of discussion, the chairperson may need to stimulate decision-making by calling for a vote. If there are time constraints on the meeting, the chairperson should be aware of these and truncate discussion when necessary. The chairperson should occasionally summarize what has been decided to that point and indicate what the group has left to do. When all the goals of the discussion have been reached, the chairperson needs to be able to summarize them and indicate what will then happen in the future.

Participation in a One-Time Meeting

Individuals who participate in a one-time meeting need to be conscious of the particular characteristics of this kind of discussion. They should not waste any time worrying about their personal concerns or role within the group, but should focus their efforts on the achievements of group goals. Participants need to maintain an open mind during discussion and keep their own contributions on topic. In a one-time meeting, it is important that all perspectives receive an airing, so participants should avoid dominating discussion. In general, participants should maintain a civil and respectful tone in their remarks, as a one-time meeting group is typically made up of individuals who do not know each other very well and they must necessarily maintain a decent rapport in order to achieve their mission

Group Discussion

Attention Span of a Small Group

One of the obstacles any small discussion group will face is the limited attention span of its members. Sometimes a discussion veers off in a direction only interesting to one or two of the group members, causing the other members to lose interest and become disengaged from the discussion. If a designated group leader exists, it is his or her job to make sure digressions are avoided and all members of the group are engaged. After the group has fully discussed a subject and can no longer continue with the topic, the group leader needs to summarize the positions of the group members and introduce a new topic for discussion. This is especially true when a group has only limited time for discussion or numerous things on the agenda.

Relationship Between Freedom and Structure in Small-Group Meetings

In their consideration of small group discussions, speech communication instructors often focus on the balance between freedom and structure. To be effective, a discussion needs to have a discernible and appropriate structure. On the other hand, to be engaging, a discussion needs to allow group members to follow their own ideas and interests. How effective a group leader is at maintaining the balance between freedom and structure will spell the difference between success and failure. With experience, discussion leaders can learn to moderate in such a way that the goals of the group are accomplished without repressing the interests of the participants. Occasionally, a group leader must refer members of the group back to the original goals, or at least reframe the current discussion in light of the avowed intentions of the group.

Benefits of Small Group Conversation

Small group conversation has a number of potential benefits. For one thing, information can be exchanged during these discussions. Small group discussions are also a useful forum for individuals to share their ideas and experiences. People are often able to convey emotion much more effectively in a small group discussion setting than through writing or communication with a larger group. A small group discussion is an excellent way to develop individual speaking and listening skills, since it is likely that each member of the group will be called upon to contribute frequently. Furthermore, a small group discussion is an ideal environment for persuading others of something because the intimacy afforded by the limited membership is conducive to building rapport.

Certain individuals seem to thrive in small group discussions. Although the charismatic qualities that make for effective small group discussion may seem abstract to many people, they are actually quite simple. For one thing, good discussion members are always sincere in what they say. They do not make the other members of the discussion group guess whether they are being serious or not. Good discussion members are also versatile and can adjust their comments and questions depending on the flow of conversation. Good discussion members exercise tact and courtesy in regard to their peers. Finally, good discussion members are good listeners, capable of demonstrating through their actions and responses that they take all the other members of the group seriously.

Group Discussions Can Help Provide Information

Group discussions are a useful source of information. The various members of a group discussion will naturally have different levels of experience and expertise on the subject at hand and will hopefully be able to fill in gaps in each other's knowledge base. Indeed, many discussion groups are organized simply for the purpose of assembling a comprehensive body of knowledge on a particular subject. It is always useful to ask participants to prepare for group discussions that have information-gathering as their explicit purpose. Sometimes a group discussion will begin by compiling all the information on the subject, after which it will move into the analysis and evaluation phases.

Group Discussions Can Yield Solid Evaluations

Group discussions are often used to evaluate a given subject. This is especially the case when the members of the group discussion are attempting to solve a particular problem. In this scenario, the group may outline the problem, describe the various proposed solutions, and then evaluate them. A small group discussion is most effective at evaluation when all the members have equal standing. Also, evaluation is most effective when all the members have a similar body of knowledge on the subject. If only a few people in the small group truly understand the problem, they may be the only ones who can contribute meaningful evaluations of the proposed solutions.

Decisions Are Made in a Group Discussion

Group discussions are often used to make decisions. Often, a group will gather and compile a body of information, evaluate potential solutions to a problem, and then decide on a course of action. Group discussions that are intended to end with decision-making seem to work best when there is an established and agreed-upon format for this process. For instance, many groups adopt parliamentary procedure as a way of organizing a discussion. For many groups, though, this may be excessively formal. In a small group, any system of decision-making is fine as long as it is agreed upon by the members. In small groups, there is enough time and space for all members to contribute their opinions before holding a vote.

PANEL DISCUSSION

Panel discussions are probably the most common form of small group discussion. They typically consist of between four to eight individuals, one of whom is designated by the others as a leader. The members of a panel discussion do not prepare formal speeches in advance of the meeting. In addition, there is no prescribed order to the proceedings beyond the fact that the discussion will be led by the designated individual. Panel discussions are typically organized to discuss a specific problem or theme. They are not really the best format for decision-making. Panel discussions often occur at conferences. When this is the case, a small group may discuss an issue before a large audience and then open the floor to questions.

LECTURE FORMAT FOR GROUP DISCUSSION

A group discussion held in a lecture format always includes a clearly defined leader. The leader will deliver a long prepared speech on a given topic. Before the meeting, various members of the discussion will have been given assignments. During the course of the leader's presentation, he or she will call on the various group members to elaborate on key points or provide specific information. During the leader's presentation, group members will have the opportunity to interrupt and ask questions. Once a subject has been covered in its entirety and is understood by all discussion members, the leader will move on to another topic.

ROUNDTABLE DISCUSSION

In a roundtable discussion, there is very little hierarchy among the members. There may be an acknowledged leader, but he or she is often not responsible for providing more information or direction to the group than any other member. All the members of a roundtable discussion are expected to have done some preparation before the beginning of the meeting. This kind of meeting format is especially appropriate for groups in which all the members can be assumed to be reasonably informed and competent in the area to be discussed. Also, groups whose members have different areas of expertise often hold roundtable discussions. When this is the case, a leader might informally direct the conversation to various members as different points in the overall subject are being discussed.

PROGRESSIVE GROUP DISCUSSION

In a progressive group discussion, a large group is divided into several smaller groups. These smaller groups simultaneously discuss the various components of a larger problem. For example, one group might focus on the roots of a problem while another group might look at the consequences of possible solutions. Each member of the discussion group may be asked to be ready to discuss all subjects or each may be assigned in advance a particular aspect of the subject to discuss. Once all the small groups have come to a general consensus, the group as a whole will reconvene and one representative from each small group will present his or her group's findings to the rest of the people.

Symposium format for group discussion: In a symposium, the participants in the discussion are allotted a certain amount of time and are placed in order ahead of time. It is typical for a symposium to have a designated leader. This leader will introduce each of the participants in the discussion. All speakers in a symposium will be discoursing on the same subject or theme. The leader will often take a moment between speakers to provide a cohesive overview of what has been covered to that point. At the end of the symposium, the speaker will offer some concluding remarks. There is no prearranged interaction between the participants in a symposium, although the leader is free to open the panel to discussion at his or her discretion.

Five steps of a successful group discussion: To be productive, a group discussion must follow a logical sequence. Speech communication instructors have delineated five basic steps in successful group discussion:

1. The group defines the problem or topic to be discussed.
2. The group compiles all the information they have on the subject.
3. The group evaluates the possible solutions to the problem or possible insights to be gained from evaluating the topic.
4. The fourth step is selecting the best solution, which may require deliberation and even voting.
5. The group will outline practical ways that the agreed-upon solution can be put into action.

Introduction of New Material Can Improve Group Discussion

One sure way to improve the quality of a group discussion is to assemble a greater amount of information. One of the common fallacies of participation in a discussion is that it does not require preparation. On the contrary, discussions are only successful to the degree that the participants can offer reasoned, well-considered examples and evidence. If necessary, group members should bring published material that is relevant to the discussion. Also, group members may want to consider how the subject or problem to be discussed has impacted their personal lives. Although group members do not want to spend a great deal of time discussing their personal lives, in some cases personal experience may have a direct influence on the discussion.

By listening more carefully and creatively, participants can improve a group discussion. In a sense, group discussion is a creative, collaborative enterprise. Group members expand upon, elaborate, and modify one another's ideas until a group consensus is reached. By listening attentively, group members achieve a good understanding of what is being said by their fellow participants, and will improve their ability to modify and embellish ideas. At any given time, every group member should be able to summarize the general topic of discussion as well as what has been said so far in the discussion.

Discussion Leadership

Although group discussions are basically a democratic arrangement, it can be useful to designate a discussion leader. A leader is someone who has the special responsibility of being prepared and keeping the business of the group on track. There are three basic kinds of leaders: non-directive, directive, and supportive.

A non-directive leader participates in the group discussion like any other member. This kind of leader exercises very little control over the actions of the group. Mainly, a non-directive leader is designated just in case the group needs help getting the discussion back on track or coming to a conclusion. If the discussion flows smoothly, a non-directive leader will not have to assert him or herself.

A directive leader is assertive in controlling the activities of the group. Unlike a non-directive leader, who only leads when the discussion gets off track, a directive leader is constantly arranging the activities of the group. A directive leader initiates discussion, calls upon members of the group to speak, and suspends discussion when he or she believes it is time. Directive leaders are more appropriate in situations where group participants are unfamiliar with one another or unfamiliar with the general dynamics of group discussion.

A supportive leader exhibits elements of both directive and non-directive leadership. The supportive leader is a bit more hands-on than a non-directive leader but is less assertive than a directive leader. Basically, a supportive leader is responsible for suggesting possible solutions and discussion strategies to the group. A supportive leader does not attempt to influence the course of discussion or the decisions made by the group, but rather seeks to aid the group in whatever direction is chosen. Supportive leaders are appropriate for groups that understand the topic thoroughly but may need some help coming to a decision.

Discussion Leader

A discussion leader is responsible for opening and closing a discussion meeting. The leader should first introduce the topic or problem to be discussed. If the members of the discussion group do not know one another, the leader should take a moment to introduce all members or allow new members to introduce themselves. The discussion leader should always make sure that every member of the discussion group fully understands the problem or topics to be discussed. Once a resolution to the problem has been found or the topic has been fully discussed, the leader should close the discussion. At this time, the leader should offer a brief summary of what has been discussed as well as the agreed-upon solution. The leader should also ask if there are any remaining questions from members of the group.

To lead a discussion group effectively, the group leader must be well prepared. Of course, all members of the discussion group need to be prepared in order to contribute in a positive way to the discussion, but this is even truer of the group leader. A leader needs to be able to summarize the topic at the beginning of the meeting and should have a rough idea of the potential solutions or conclusions the group will come up with. A leader must also be fluent enough in the discussion topic to summarize it to the group at various points during the discussion.

It is imperative for a group leader to maintain the focus of the group on the task at hand. All too often, a group discussion goes off down a blind alley or ends up in unproductive digressions. Even a non-directive leader needs to be capable of stepping in and refocusing the attention of the group one easy way to do this is by restating or summarizing what has been discussed so far. This tends to draw the attention of the group members back to the original task at hand. A group leader may also indicate discussion topics that still need to be addressed or try to refocus the group by asking a general question about the central issue of the discussion.

Discussion Critique Can Be Performed

After a discussion is over, it is advantageous to spend some time considering which aspects of it were successful and which were not. To this end, many people find it useful to complete a discussion critique. A discussion critique is simply a standardized form on which people can indicate their opinion of the discussion. Sometimes, participants are asked to grade the quality of discussion in a number of different areas on a scale of one to ten. Some discussion critique forms ask participants to grade the individual performances of their fellow group members. When this is the case, it may be appropriate to make the forms anonymous.

Use of Interaction and Participation Diagrams

People who study group discussion often use participation and interaction diagrams as tools for analysis and evaluation. These diagrams indicate how many times every participant in a discussion has spoken, on what issues they spoke, and to whom they directed their comments. The members of the group are represented in boxes or circles on the form. Lines drawn between the participants indicate interactions during the discussion. These diagrams can be useful because they indicate when certain members of the group are primarily talking amongst themselves as opposed to involving all the members of the group. Sometimes a group leader will study interaction and participation diagrams and realize that conversation has been unfairly dominated by a few members of the group.

Oral Communication Builds Community

Public speaking is an act that creates and reinforces the bonds of a community. When a person speaks in public, he or she is expressing his or her own opinions and beliefs, which may echo or stand in contrast to those of the community. In either case, public speech requires the listeners to consider their own shared beliefs. Public speech draws attention to the similarities and differences between various communities through a process known as cultural maintenance. Through the creation of a public discourse, the members of a community learn about each other and think critically about their social mores and cultural values.

Media and Mass Communication

Development of Radio Communication

At one point in American history, radio communication was the most important means of mass communication. The first commercial radio station began broadcasting in 1920. At first, radio was not very popular, because most people could not afford home receivers. As these devices began to become more common in American homes, however, programming expanded and the radio became a source of information and entertainment. In 1941, the first FM station began broadcasting, allowing signals to be transmitted over long distances with a very small amount of static. Although radio communication has been somewhat superseded by television and the Internet, it is still an invaluable source of information and entertainment for millions of people

Relationship of Radio to Other Forms of Mass Media

When it was first introduced, radio was the most important form of mass communication. Unlike telegraphs, radios could deliver complex messages about events as they happened. Also, radio allowed for dramatic use of the human voice and special sound effects. In general, radio is a more personal medium than telegraph communication. Eventually, however, the ability of television to transmit images and sound allowed this medium to supersede radio as the primary form of mass communication. Nevertheless, radio remains the predominant medium for the transmission of music and continues to be an important vehicle for the transmission of news.

Development of radio networks: One of the most important periods in the history of radio communication was the development of radio networks. Radio networks first developed as a way to offset the costs of maintaining radio towers and transmission equipment. Radio networks began to sell commercials to businesses that wanted to advertise. These businesses would pay the radio station for the right to air their advertisements. Various radio stations joined together in networks and gave one another permission to air each other's shows. In this way, radio stations around the country standardized programming and made radio a viable business. Each station was able to produce a smaller amount

Development of Motion Pictures

The first motion pictures were developed by Thomas Edison and his associates in 1893. After a few years of tinkering, motion pictures were introduced to the general public and were immediately popular. Many stores offered "nickelodeons," in which patrons could watch a brief presentation for a nickel. Around 1910, a small film industry began to develop in Hollywood, California. In 1912, the first full-size theaters were introduced. In the mid-1920s, sound was added to motion pictures, which had previously been silent or accompanied by live music. By 1929, all new films had sound.

Significance of motion pictures: Motion pictures have played an important role in the economic and social life of the United States. Perhaps the first example of the effect of the movies was during the Great Depression, when motion pictures continued to portray images of success and wealth in spite of the widespread poverty beyond the theater. It was at this point that people began to note the escapism inherent in the movie-watching experience. Since then movies have proven to be a powerful medium for exploring real events, including tragic ones. Two good examples of this are the newsreels of battle footage from World War II and the many powerful movies that have been made on the subject of the Vietnam War.

Development of Television Communication

Television is such an entrenched part of daily American life that some might forget that it has really only been part of the culture for the past sixty years. Although the first television broadcasts took place in 1939, it was only after World War II that television truly burst onto the American scene. At first, televisions were extremely expensive and signals were only broadcast in black and white. Also, when televisions were first introduced, radio communication was still the most popular medium. Over time, however, televisions became smaller and less expensive and better quality programming became available. After approximately a decade, television supplanted radio as the most popular form of mass communication in the United States.

Television provides news coverage: Because of its ability to deliver visual images and sound, television has proven to be an excellent medium for transmitting news. Many people get the majority of their information from television broadcasts. Television transmission has allowed people to get global news and learn about life in even the farthest reaches of the world, which they might otherwise never be able to see or visit. At the same time, many television news programs seek to provide in-depth analysis and evaluation of local, state, federal, and global issues. Television has proven to be an excellent medium for interviews and documentaries as well.

Television provides entertainment: For most people, television is primarily a source of entertainment. Comedies, sports, dramas, game shows, and reality programs are among the most popular forms of television entertainment. Perhaps the most venerable form of television entertainment is the soap opera, so named because the first programs targeted housewives and were sponsored by soap companies. Some television programs air at a regular time for years on end, while others, such as miniseries, are only on the air for a limited time. Television executives determine which entertainment shows they will continue broadcasting by evaluating Nielsen ratings, which measure how many viewers are tuning in to each program.

Relationship Between Television and Business

Over time, television has become a big business. Television stations make most of their money by airing commercials. Although television stations must pay for their transmission equipment, their primary expenditure is for the development of programming. Television networks, similar to radio networks, developed as a way to share the costs of program development. Broadcast television, which is available simply with the use of an antenna, is free to the general public. Cable television, on the other hand, must be purchased by subscription. The advent of cable television in the 1950s allowed television stations to fund special-interest programming for a limited audience.

Media's Role in Informing the Public

The mass media plays a central role in informing the general public about local and global events. When most people think about information disseminated through the media, they think about news programming. But there are a number of other venues through which information is transmitted to the public. For instance, nature documentaries and talk shows inform the general public on issues that are perhaps less immediately pertinent to their lives. The federal government uses channels of communication such as radio and television to broadcast emergency messages and to promote governmental policies. Magazines and newspapers can also disseminate detailed information on behalf of government agencies.

Media's Role in Changing Attitudes and Behavior

Although the precise power of the media is a matter of controversy, it is beyond question that the major media outlets have an ability to persuade the general public. To take the most obvious example, advertisements on television clearly have a positive effect on sales. Many of the ways in which the media can influence attitudes and behavior are more subtle, however. For instance, simply by providing information about a particular subject, the media can influence popular opinion. One indication of the media's influence on behavior is shown simply in the fact that people commonly choose to spend time watching television or listening to the radio rather than doing other things.

Media's Role in Entertaining the Public

In public surveys, people cite entertainment as the number one reason for engaging with mass media. This data is produced by Nielsen ratings, which indicate that people watch sports, comedy, and drama programming much more frequently than news. Moreover, the line between information and entertainment is often blurred. For instance, many documentaries that purport to be informative are also quite entertaining. Indeed, the inherently entertaining nature of mass media communication makes such media a powerful tool for engaging an audience in educational and informative programming. Many people acquire a broad knowledge of the world through television and radio without ever realizing they are engaged in a process of education.

Development of the Internet and Its Effect on Communication

Although the Internet has been around for approximately 20 years, it did not truly become part of the mainstream media until the mid-1990s. Today it is ubiquitous within American culture and is an integral part of the way people communicate with one another. Instantaneous forms of communication such as E-mail, instant messaging, blogging, and video blogging and conferencing have all become available to people who formerly would have had no access to them. The result is that it is now possible to communicate with people around the globe at virtually any time. The Internet has brought formerly isolated geographic areas into contact with other parts of the world and has provided forums for members of every special-interest group in existence. At the same time, many critics charge that the instantaneous communication afforded by the Internet has impoverished communication on the local and community level.

Media

Mass communication is defined as the one-way transmission of messages to a large, diverse audience. Radio, television, and the Internet are the typical vehicles for mass communication. Some people include print media as a component of mass communication, although others declare that mass media requires almost instantaneous transmission. One of the signature qualities of mass media communication is that it can be reproduced and replayed in exactly the same way more than once. In other words, since it has the capability of being recorded, it can be played more than once and for more than one audience.

Use of a Media Diary

Many people would be shocked to realize just how much time they spend engaged with mass media. Spending a half-hour here, forty-five minutes there in total can add up to a huge chunk of time. One way to gain control over the time spent engaged with mass media is to maintain a media diary. A media diary is simply a daily catalog of the amount of time devoted to different forms of media. For instance, a student might want to keep a media diary listing the amount of time spent listening to the radio, watching television, or surfing the Internet. It might also be a good idea to include activities such as watching movies and playing video games. Students should record how much time they spend in each one of these activities and then calculate it as a percentage of their total free time.

Use of a Media Evaluation Form

Another way to keep track of individual media intake is through the use of a media evaluation form. Unlike a media diary, which simply indicates how much time was spent with various media, a media evaluation form keeps track of the quality and content of the media that is consumed. For instance, a media evaluation form will include a list of the various television programs the individual watched during the week, along with a brief summary and evaluation of the programs. Many people are shocked to discover how much time they spend every week engaged with programming they do not particularly enjoy. The use of the media evaluation form is a great way to streamline media intake because it encourages an individual to devote time only to content he or she most enjoys.

Media's Ability to Spur Public Conversation

One of the key roles of the mass media is to inspire and shape public dialogue. For instance, the news media's coverage of a political issue can set up debate. Many people have alleged over the years that the news media in the United States has a particular political bias. Some people claim it has a liberal bias, while others claim it is a conservative bias. Perhaps the safest criticism one can make of the news media is that it has an inherent interest in conflict, because controversy and disagreement is more interesting to viewers. Most critics of the mass media agree that it is influenced in large part by the desire to sell advertising space.

Media's Ability to Frame Discussion

One of the media's greatest responsibilities is to frame public discussion in a fair and objective way. In other words, the media is charged with reporting the news in a way that gives ample space to all reasonable points of view and does not ignore pertinent facts on either side. The role of the media in influencing discussion in a society has led some critics to refer to news outlets as "information gatekeepers." It is important that there be vocal critics of the news media, to identify and remedy problems of objectivity to a certain degree, all citizens are responsible for casting a skeptical eye on the news media and for making sure these media enable free and fair discussion.

Importance of Applying Critical Analysis Skills to the Media

When the news media is free and unfettered, it is essential for all citizens to maintain a skeptical attitude and apply critical analysis skills to informative programming. Television viewers should keep in mind that the way a subject is photographed can influence the way it is perceived. For instance, individuals who are photographed in shadow tend to seem more dangerous or malevolent. Most people are good at critically appraising commercials but do not necessarily apply the same skills to avowedly informative programming. Viewers should remember that a persuasive element exists in every communication, no matter how impartial, and so should remain alert to signs of bias.

General Feedback is Offered to the Media

The providers of mass media communication receive general feedback from a number of different sources. Television companies, for instance, are constantly organizing focus groups to view and offer feedback on new television shows and commercials. Sometimes networks will arrange for a focus group to be composed entirely of members of a particular demographic, as for example women or African-Americans. Perhaps the most famous example of general feedback for the mass media is the Nielsen ratings, which are used to determine how many people watch a particular television program. The providers of mass communication use all of this general feedback to refine and tailor their messages to the audience.

Personal Feedback is Offered to the Media

The media receives a great deal of personal feedback from individuals in the general public. Any time a person writes or calls a television or radio station to convey his or her response to a program, he or she is giving personal feedback. Many television and radio programs explicitly call for audience participation, which is to say they ask for personal feedback to use as content in their programming. In a way, consumers provide personal feedback to the media in their choice of purchases, since these consumer decisions indicate which television and radio advertisements are effective. Individual voices actually do play a great role in affecting the quality of the content of media presentations.

Programming Process for Radio and Television

Radio and television programming is primarily a matter of economics. Networks want to schedule their most expensive and most popular programming at the times when the most people are likely to see or hear it. For radio this means during the morning and afternoon, when people are likely to be in their cars, whereas for television this means the early evening hours. New television dramas and comedies are usually introduced twice a year. Networks usually produce from ten to fifteen new episodes in each television season. A show may have two seasons in a year and during the remaining weeks reruns will be broadcast. Traditionally, news programs are broadcast in the early morning, at noon, around dinnertime, and in the late evening.

Media Outlets are Funded

In large part, television and radio networks are funded by commercials. The Nielsen ratings indicate how many viewers watch a particular television program. The more viewers a program receives, the more expensive is the advertising space during the program. Every year, the Super Bowl marks the most expensive four hours of programming on American television, with some 30-second advertising slots going for more than one million dollars. There are alternatives to advertising-funded television and radio, such as public television and radio stations, which are primarily funded by viewer donations and contributions from grant organizations. Also, some small public access television stations are funded by their local government.

Use of Commercials in Mass Communication

Nearly all programming on radio and broadcast television is funded by commercials. Cable and satellite television receive part of their funding from distributors but are in large part also funded by advertising. Commercials are generally more expensive when they run during programs with a large viewership. Businesses also like to position their advertising during programs that attract viewers who are likely to buy their products. So, for instance, one is likely to see a lot of truck commercials during football games, since presumably a large number of males are watching. Similarly, commercials during the weekdays are often for products preferred by senior citizens and housewives, who are more likely to be watching television at this time.

Advances in Mass Communication Have Changed the Legislative Process

In the past fifty years, the legislative process has been subtly modified by advances in communication technology. Television first made it possible for the president to speak face to face, as it were, with the American public. This meant he could push his legislative agenda without having to spend as much time currying favor among members of Congress. Perhaps the most important change has been the introduction of C-Span, a network that televises all the proceedings in the US Senate and House of Representatives. This has made members of Congress even more conscious of their appearance and has led to much more grandstanding and many more public displays on the floor of the legislature. Also, the acceleration of the news cycle has put perhaps unfair pressure on Congress to move quickly on legislative decisions.

Internet's Effect on Politics

The Internet has influenced politics in unpredictable ways. For one thing, it has made it possible for citizens to acquire political information from sources other than the traditional mainstream media. In the past, many people have complained about the prejudices of the news media, but now people are easily able to get news from sources that share their same personal ideologies. Many people complain, however, that this "hyper-partisanship" of many Internet news sources has polarized the country. Another area in which the Internet has radically changed politics is in campaign financing. Candidates can now solicit donations over the Internet, which has led to amazing increases in the amount of money available to popular candidates.

Communication Media Affects the Political Campaign Process

Advances in communication technology have drastically altered the political process. Before the advent of television, political candidates could only reach large audiences on the radio or by delivering addresses to enormous crowds. The development of broadcast television made it possible for presidential debates to be transmitted to the entire country. At the same time, candidates began to pay much more attention to the visual elements of presentation. With the introduction of the first 24-hour cable news networks, it became more and more important for ambitious politicians to supply ready-made news events. This has spawned the omnipresent, continuous cycle of political news and campaign coverage. Many critics complain that the incessant need for fresh news by the cable networks has devalued political discourse in the United States, even as these networks provide information to many more people than were reached in the past.

Radio Drama

Vocal Techniques Used in Radio Drama

Some of the best oral interpretation of famous stories and plays has been done over the radio. For oral interpretation to work on the radio, however, the performers must have excellent vocal control. For one thing, they need to be able to indicate excitement or nervousness with their rate of speech. An excited speaker tends to talk more quickly. Radio drama performers also have to indicate their emotional state by varying the volume of their voice. For instance, in many radio dramas a speaker will almost whisper during the most dramatic parts, because the audience will then be forced to listen more intently to what he or she is saying.

Preparing a Radio Drama

A great deal of effort goes into the preparation of most radio dramas. Not only do the performers need to become familiar with their roles and practice the performance, but the producers need to decide on the appropriate sound effects to accompany the performance. Like television programs and movies, radio dramas have directors, who are responsible for organizing the actors and overseeing the general interpretation of the text. Typically, a director will go through the text before auditions are even held, so he or she can get a good idea of the particular themes that should be emphasized in the performance.

Rehearsing a Radio Drama

It is just as important to rehearse a radio drama as it is to rehearse a scene in a movie, a television program, or a play. The director of a radio drama usually organizes a rehearsal right after the parts have been cast, so the group can run through the entire script together and get a general idea of the direction in which they are heading. During this rehearsal, members of the cast make notes on their scripts. In subsequent rehearsals, the director will probably interrupt the cast in order to offer suggestions and make corrections. It is typical to do a final rehearsal a short time before the premiere presentation.

Sound Effects in a Radio Drama

Radio dramas have famously been enlivened by the use of sound effects. Sound effects serve a number of purposes in the presentation of a radio drama. For one thing, they can be used to differentiate between scenes. Often, a bit of background noise helps to establish a new scene in the minds of an audience. For instance, a scene might begin with the sound of shuffling feet and low conversation, to indicate that the action is taking place in a hallway or on the street. Sound effects also add depth to a radio drama. Instead of just listening to the human voice, the audience hears a variety of noises that advance the action, from ringing telephones to slamming doors. Because radio only transmits through the medium of sound, radio drama producers have become extremely creative with the incorporation of sound effects.

Video Production Terms

Basic terminology used in video and film production includes the following:

Angle—the viewpoint from which the camera shoots the action.

Establishing shot—a shot from a long distance, used to establish the setting in the mind of the viewer; often a shot of the building in which the action takes place.

Close-up—a shot in which the camera only focuses on one person; extremely close shots are referred to as tight close-ups and extreme close-ups.

Dolly—a platform on wheels that allows a camera to remain stable while moving; used primarily in action scenes or when there is a change in perspective during a shot.

Medium shot—a camera perspective in which an individual is framed to the waist; a medium shot contains enough width for two people; sometimes used to frame people as they walk or run.

Long shot—a camera perspective in which several people can be included from head to foot; a long shot is often used to establish a conversational group at the beginning of a scene.

Wide angle—a camera perspective that has an extremely broad horizontal distance.

Reverse angle—a camera perspective in which the object being shot is seen from a perspective that is the opposite of the previous shot.

Pan—a filming technique in which the camera is turned horizontally on an axis; often used when the subject is in motion, as for instance when a character is walking.

Tilt—a camera technique in which the camera is moved up and down vertically on an axis; sometimes used to shift the frame from an individual's feet to the individual's head.

Cut—sometimes called a take; a transition from one scene to another.

Zoom—to move closer to or farther away from the subject with the camera.

Fade—a gradual dissolution of the scene; most often, movies and television shows use a fade to black.

Dissolve—a gradual transition between scenes, in which the first scene is slowly replaced by the second scene.

Wipe—a transition between scenes in which one moves in as the other moves out, with no overlap.

Over the shoulder shot—a classic camera perspective in which one individual is seen from the perspective of a point over the shoulder of another person.

Preparation of a Camera Shot Sheet

One of the most important tasks of a television or film director is to prepare a camera shot sheet. A camera shot sheet is a detailed set of instructions that the various camera operators must follow during filming. For each shot, the director should list what is to be framed, the type of lens to be used, the length of taping to be expected, and the sound requirements. All this information needs to be condensed into a format small enough for all the camera operators to carry around during shooting. It is very important that the sequence of shots be accurate, so the camera operators can spend their time preparing for their next shot.

Roles of Producer and Director in a Television Production

The producer of a television program has a variety of different roles. Perhaps most generally, the producer can be called the overall manager of the production. He or she arranges the financial backing, hires the crew, and assigns a director to the project. Once the production is underway, the producer acts as a liaison between the financial backers and the director. The producer may also have a role in assisting publicity. A television production's director is hired by the producer to interpret the script, cast the parts, and to manage the crew that will film the program. The director is responsible for creating an interpretation that is acceptable to the producer.

Roles of Associate Director, Floor Manager, and Production Assistant in a Television Production

An associate director has several tasks on the set of a television production. For one thing, the associate director is usually in charge of directing the background action. That is, he or she makes sure future shots are being set up while the director concentrates on what is being filmed at present. The associate director also tries to keep the director organized and on schedule. The associate director is often responsible for managing the logistics of production as well. The floor manager, meanwhile, is responsible for organizing the facilities that will be used in the production and for maintaining the operation schedule. A production assistant typically takes care of the finer details of production, from the making of cue cards to set design.

Microphones, Switchers, and Mixers in a Television Production

A variety of specialized equipment is required for television production. For one thing, television requires the use of hidden microphones. The most common microphone used on a television set is one suspended from a long horizontal pole, called a mike boom. The mike boom allows the microphone to be suspended above the performer but out of sight of the camera. Television production also requires the use of a switcher, which is a mixing panel that allows scenes to be placed end to end on a videotape. Finally, television production requires the use of a mixer, which is an electronic board on which various sources of sound and video can be spliced together.

Phases of Television Production

Television production includes four basic phases: preproduction planning, rehearsal, productions, and postproduction. During preproduction planning, the director familiarizes himself or herself with the script, and a production assistant arranges for the facility and the production equipment. The cast and crew are also hired at this stage. During the rehearsal phase, the actors and director figure out their roles and do the blocking. During the production phase, the program is filmed. Finally, during the all-important postproduction period, the program is edited and mixed. Also during this period corrections are made, art and music are added, and any necessary dubbing is performed.

Use of a Personal Media Inventory

A personal media inventory is a record of one's media intake over a given period of time. A comprehensive personal media inventory would include categories for television, radio, movies, Internet, recorded music, and any other form of mass media. Most people are very surprised when they realize how much time they actually spend engaged with media. In particular, many people are shocked to realize just how much television they watch each week. One way to gain control over the amount of time one spends with mass media is to catalog this activity in a personal media inventory.

DSST Practice Test

1. Which of the following is not an effective listening technique?

a. Interrupt to ask questions; paraphrase
b. Focus; don't form opinions too soon
c. Lean forward; tap on the table
d. Make eye contact; avoid being defensive
e. Nod and mirror the body language of the speaker

2. Which of the following series lists the elements of effective communication?

a. Sender, receiver, message, channel, feedback
b. Sender, receiver, message, direction, response
c. Speaker, listener, point, medium, reaction
d. Speaker, respondent, purpose, route, organization
e. To, from, directionality, reason, accomplishment

3. Broadly speaking, in our culture personal space is typically ____, while social space is ____. Of these types of spaces, ____ is more likely to affect how communication is shaped.

a. 0-3 feet; 4-12 feet; social space
b. 1 ½-4 feet; 4-12 feet; personal space
c. 1 ½-4 feet; 4-12 feet; social space
d. 0-3 feet; 4-12 feet; personal space
e. 1 ½-4 feet; 3-7 feet; personal space

4. Which type of nonverbal message deals with belonging, control, respect, or disapproval?

a. Emotive messages
b. Relational messages
c. Content messages
d. Interpersonal messages
e. Intrapersonal messages

5. What is involved in language comprehension?

a. Hearing sounds, processing words and organizing them
b. Hearing sounds and understanding their meanings
c. Speaking the same language as the sender
d. Identifying word units, knowing their meanings, understanding their syntactical use, processing abstractions, interpreting meaning
e. Understanding complex ideas, interpreting meaning

6. To what degree is effective listening natural to all people?

a. An innate ability to listen effectively is inborn.
b. An innate ability to listen effectively is inborn for some people.
c. An innate ability to listen effectively is inborn, but is quickly lost if not nurtured.
d. An innate ability to listen effectively is inborn for some people, but will be lost if not nurtured by age three.
e. An innate ability to listen effectively is not a natural skill.

7. Expressive language competency requires all of the following except:

a. Oral language
b. Gesture
c. Tone
d. Context
e. Written language

8. The best way to emphasize an important point in a public presentation is:

a. Prepare the audience by telling them you are about to reveal a key point.
b. Speak more quickly to attract the audience's attention.
c. Speak more slowly to give the audience time to consider what is being said.
d. Pause for a long moment before delivering the point.
e. Speak loudly to alert those whose minds are drifting.

9. Within a classroom setting, the reason for a debate is:

a. To determine which side has the most correct answers
b. To teach students to research, collaborate, argue, and listen
c. To demonstrate to students that there is no ultimate truth
d. To cast doubt on the other side's position
e. To convince students to change opinions

10. The earliest known writing on dramatic theory was:

a. Plato's poetics
b. Aristotle's poetics
c. Virgil's poetics
d. Virgil's dramatica
e. Plato's allegories

Answer Key and Explanations

1. C: Listening effectively requires the conscious use of a number of skills. First, the listener should focus on what's being said. The listener can show the speaker she's being heard by making eye contact or leaning forward. Forming an early opinion or judgment can cause a misinterpretation of the intended message, and becoming defensive shuts down an open mind. Paraphrasing and asking questions can help clarify the speaker's intended meaning. Paying attention to tone of voice, inflection, mood, or emotion is also an effective listening technique because they contribute to the message. Mirroring also communicates engaged listening. Tapping on the table (c) is not an effective listening technique.

2. A: In both writing and speaking, effective communication involves a sender who initiates the communication and a receiver (audience) for whom it's intended. The message is the communication that is received, which may be different from what was intended. The channel is the medium by which the message travels. It might be an e-mail, a presentation, a commercial, or a verbal exchange. Feedback is how the receiver responds, and helps the sender know if the message arrived intact.

3. B: The environment in which a communication is initiated and received plays an important role in how that communication manifests, both because the environmental context contributes to meaning by offering reference, and because the environment can enhance or detract from the receiver's ability to process the message. Personal space (about 1 ½ - 4 feet) has a greater bearing on the formation or receipt of the message than does social space (about 4 – 12 feet). It's important to recognize that both social and personal space vary from culture to culture; what is acceptable in one may not be in another.

4. B: Relational messages, as opposed to content messages, are concerned with the relationship between a speaker and a recipient rather than with the overt subject of the communication. They may convey belonging, respect, or disapproval, among other things. They are frequently largely or entirely nonverbal; because of this, they may be supported with verbal feedback to confirm them. The content of the message, "Should I come over after work?" is a logistical request. If a speaker leans forward to touch a recipient who is weeping, the relational message is "Do you need my support?" The recipient might respond with a nod and a grateful look, or might clarify the speaker's offer by saying, "I won't be good company, but you can come."

5. D: Language comprehension doesn't necessarily involve sounds or speaking. For example, sign language and written language use different materials to form words. It does, however, require identifying words, knowing their meanings, recognizing how they are being used in the context of a sentence, understanding abstractions such as idioms or references, and drawing a conclusion regarding the message's meaning.

6. E: Listening is an essential communication skill. In any type of communication, participants spend a substantially greater amount of time listening than speaking. Listening is a learned skill as opposed to a natural, innate ability. Children learn to listen by modeling behaviors demonstrated by others and by practicing. They quickly learn that listening to tone, speed, and volume can offer important nonverbal clues about the overall meaning of a message.

7. E: Expressive language competency is the ability to express oneself orally, not in writing. In order to use expressive language capably, the speaker must have control over nonverbal as well as verbal aspects of language. First, he or she must obviously know how to use oral language. Body language and gestures can add to or clarify the meaning of an oral message. For instance, turning away suggests dismissal, while leaning toward the recipient suggests inclusion. The tone in which a statement is made can indicate irony, satire, or enthusiasm. It can also introduce emotional or psychological overtones. The context in which a statement is made also affects meaning.

8. D: Before delivering a central point in a speech, the speaker should stop talking for a moment. During that moment of silence, however, it's important not to disengage. Instead, the speaker should make eye contact, lean or step forward, take an audible deep breath, raise his or her eyebrows, or use other nonverbal methods to alert the audience that what follows is important.

9. B: Debate is a highly useful classroom technique in that it teaches the skills necessary for communication. Each participant must conduct research and consider what he or she knows about the subject; work collaboratively with other students to clarify beliefs and positions; present an argument that is logical, lucid, and on-point; listen to the response as well as to the other team's message; and respond when appropriate.

10. B: Aristotle's poetics, written around 335 B.C., is a philosophical text concerned with dramatic presentations and poetry. Poetic genres are categorized in terms of the vehicle of language (language, harmony, and rhythm); objects [agents (actors or symbolic objects) and actions]; and their representative modes, specifically tragedy, comedy, lyric poetry, epic poetry, and dithyramb, a hymn sung and danced by performers.

How to Overcome Test Anxiety

Just the thought of taking a test is enough to make most people a little nervous. A test is an important event that can have a long-term impact on your future, so it's important to take it seriously and it's natural to feel anxious about performing well. But just because anxiety is normal, that doesn't mean that it's helpful in test taking, or that you should simply accept it as part of your life. Anxiety can have a variety of effects. These effects can be mild, like making you feel slightly nervous, or severe, like blocking your ability to focus or remember even a simple detail.

If you experience test anxiety—whether severe or mild—it's important to know how to beat it. To discover this, first you need to understand what causes test anxiety.

Causes of Test Anxiety

While we often think of anxiety as an uncontrollable emotional state, it can actually be caused by simple, practical things. One of the most common causes of test anxiety is that a person does not feel adequately prepared for their test. This feeling can be the result of many different issues such as poor study habits or lack of organization, but the most common culprit is time management. Starting to study too late, failing to organize your study time to cover all of the material, or being distracted while you study will mean that you're not well prepared for the test. This may lead to cramming the night before, which will cause you to be physically and mentally exhausted for the test. Poor time management also contributes to feelings of stress, fear, and hopelessness as you realize you are not well prepared but don't know what to do about it.

Other times, test anxiety is not related to your preparation for the test but comes from unresolved fear. This may be a past failure on a test, or poor performance on tests in general. It may come from comparing yourself to others who seem to be performing better or from the stress of living up to expectations. Anxiety may be driven by fears of the future—how failure on this test would affect your educational and career goals. These fears are often completely irrational, but they can still negatively impact your test performance.

Elements of Test Anxiety

As mentioned earlier, test anxiety is considered to be an emotional state, but it has physical and mental components as well. Sometimes you may not even realize that you are suffering from test anxiety until you notice the physical symptoms. These can include trembling hands, rapid heartbeat, sweating, nausea, and tense muscles. Extreme anxiety may lead to fainting or vomiting. Obviously, any of these symptoms can have a negative impact on testing. It is important to recognize them as soon as they begin to occur so that you can address the problem before it damages your performance.

The mental components of test anxiety include trouble focusing and inability to remember learned information. During a test, your mind is on high alert, which can help you recall information and stay focused for an extended period of time. However, anxiety interferes with your mind's natural processes, causing you to blank out, even on the questions you know well. The strain of testing during anxiety makes it difficult to stay focused, especially on a test that may take several hours. Extreme anxiety can take a huge mental toll, making it difficult not only to recall test information but even to understand the test questions or pull your thoughts together.

Effects of Test Anxiety

Test anxiety is like a disease—if left untreated, it will get progressively worse. Anxiety leads to poor performance, and this reinforces the feelings of fear and failure, which in turn lead to poor performances on subsequent tests. It can grow from a mild nervousness to a crippling condition. If allowed to progress, test anxiety can have a big impact on your schooling, and consequently on your future.

Test anxiety can spread to other parts of your life. Anxiety on tests can become anxiety in any stressful situation, and blanking on a test can turn into panicking in a job situation. But fortunately, you don't have to let anxiety rule your testing and determine your grades. There are a number of relatively simple steps you can take to move past anxiety and function normally on a test and in the rest of life.

Physical Steps for Beating Test Anxiety

While test anxiety is a serious problem, the good news is that it can be overcome. It doesn't have to control your ability to think and remember information. While it may take time, you can begin taking steps today to beat anxiety.

Just as your first hint that you may be struggling with anxiety comes from the physical symptoms, the first step to treating it is also physical. Rest is crucial for having a clear, strong mind. If you are tired, it is much easier to give in to anxiety. But if you establish good sleep habits, your body and mind will be ready to perform optimally, without the strain of exhaustion. Additionally, sleeping well helps you to retain information better, so you're more likely to recall the answers when you see the test questions.

Getting good sleep means more than going to bed on time. It's important to allow your brain time to relax. Take study breaks from time to time so it doesn't get overworked, and don't study right before bed. Take time to rest your mind before trying to rest your body, or you may find it difficult to fall asleep.

Along with sleep, other aspects of physical health are important in preparing for a test. Good nutrition is vital for good brain function. Sugary foods and drinks may give a burst of energy but this burst is followed by a crash, both physically and emotionally. Instead, fuel your body with protein and vitamin-rich foods.

Also, drink plenty of water. Dehydration can lead to headaches and exhaustion, especially if your brain is already under stress from the rigors of the test. Particularly if your test is a long one, drink water during the breaks. And if possible, take an energy-boosting snack to eat between sections.

Along with sleep and diet, a third important part of physical health is exercise. Maintaining a steady workout schedule is helpful, but even taking 5-minute study breaks to walk can help get your blood pumping faster and clear your head. Exercise also releases endorphins, which contribute to a positive feeling and can help combat test anxiety.

When you nurture your physical health, you are also contributing to your mental health. If your body is healthy, your mind is much more likely to be healthy as well. So take time to rest, nourish your body with healthy food and water, and get moving as much as possible. Taking these physical steps will make you stronger and more able to take the mental steps necessary to overcome test anxiety.

Mental Steps for Beating Test Anxiety

Working on the mental side of test anxiety can be more challenging, but as with the physical side, there are clear steps you can take to overcome it. As mentioned earlier, test anxiety often stems from lack of preparation, so the obvious solution is to prepare for the test. Effective studying may be the most important weapon you have for beating test anxiety, but you can and should employ several other mental tools to combat fear.

First, boost your confidence by reminding yourself of past success—tests or projects that you aced. If you're putting as much effort into preparing for this test as you did for those, there's no reason you should expect to fail here. Work hard to prepare; then trust your preparation.

Second, surround yourself with encouraging people. It can be helpful to find a study group, but be sure that the people you're around will encourage a positive attitude. If you spend time with others who are anxious or cynical, this will only contribute to your own anxiety. Look for others who are motivated to study hard from a desire to succeed, not from a fear of failure.

Third, reward yourself. A test is physically and mentally tiring, even without anxiety, and it can be helpful to have something to look forward to. Plan an activity following the test, regardless of the outcome, such as going to a movie or getting ice cream.

When you are taking the test, if you find yourself beginning to feel anxious, remind yourself that you know the material. Visualize successfully completing the test. Then take a few deep, relaxing breaths and return to it. Work through the questions carefully but with confidence, knowing that you are capable of succeeding.

Developing a healthy mental approach to test taking will also aid in other areas of life. Test anxiety affects more than just the actual test—it can be damaging to your mental health and even contribute to depression. It's important to beat test anxiety before it becomes a problem for more than testing.

Study Strategy

Being prepared for the test is necessary to combat anxiety, but what does being prepared look like? You may study for hours on end and still not feel prepared. What you need is a strategy for test prep. The next few pages outline our recommended steps to help you plan out and conquer the challenge of preparation.

Step 1: Scope Out the Test

Learn everything you can about the format (multiple choice, essay, etc.) and what will be on the test. Gather any study materials, course outlines, or sample exams that may be available. Not only will this help you to prepare, but knowing what to expect can help to alleviate test anxiety.

Step 2: Map Out the Material

Look through the textbook or study guide and make note of how many chapters or sections it has. Then divide these over the time you have. For example, if a book has 15 chapters and you have five days to study, you need to cover three chapters each day. Even better, if you have the time, leave an extra day at the end for overall review after you have gone through the material in depth.

If time is limited, you may need to prioritize the material. Look through it and make note of which sections you think you already have a good grasp on, and which need review. While you are studying, skim quickly through the familiar sections and take more time on the challenging parts.

Write out your plan so you don't get lost as you go. Having a written plan also helps you feel more in control of the study, so anxiety is less likely to arise from feeling overwhelmed at the amount to cover.

Step 3: Gather Your Tools

Decide what study method works best for you. Do you prefer to highlight in the book as you study and then go back over the highlighted portions? Or do you type out notes of the important information? Or is it helpful to make flashcards that you can carry with you? Assemble the pens, index cards, highlighters, post-it notes, and any other materials you may need so you won't be distracted by getting up to find things while you study.

If you're having a hard time retaining the information or organizing your notes, experiment with different methods. For example, try color-coding by subject with colored pens, highlighters, or post-it notes. If you learn better by hearing, try recording yourself reading your notes so you can listen while in the car, working out, or simply sitting at your desk. Ask a friend to quiz you from your flashcards, or try teaching someone the material to solidify it in your mind.

Step 4: Create Your Environment

It's important to avoid distractions while you study. This includes both the obvious distractions like visitors and the subtle distractions like an uncomfortable chair (or a too-comfortable couch that makes you want to fall asleep). Set up the best study environment possible: good lighting and a comfortable work area. If background music helps you focus, you may want to turn it on, but otherwise keep the room quiet. If you are using a computer to take notes, be sure you don't have any other windows open, especially applications like social media, games, or anything else that could distract you. Silence your phone and turn off notifications. Be sure to keep water close by so you stay hydrated while you study (but avoid unhealthy drinks and snacks).

Also, take into account the best time of day to study. Are you freshest first thing in the morning? Try to set aside some time then to work through the material. Is your mind clearer in the afternoon or evening? Schedule your study session then. Another method is to study at the same time of day that you will take the test, so that your brain gets used to working on the material at that time and will be ready to focus at test time.

Step 5: Study!

Once you have done all the study preparation, it's time to settle into the actual studying. Sit down, take a few moments to settle your mind so you can focus, and begin to follow your study plan. Don't give in to distractions or let yourself procrastinate. This is your time to prepare so you'll be ready to fearlessly approach the test. Make the most of the time and stay focused.

Of course, you don't want to burn out. If you study too long you may find that you're not retaining the information very well. Take regular study breaks. For example, taking five minutes out of every hour to walk briskly, breathing deeply and swinging your arms, can help your mind stay fresh.

As you get to the end of each chapter or section, it's a good idea to do a quick review. Remind yourself of what you learned and work on any difficult parts. When you feel that you've mastered the material, move on to the next part. At the end of your study session, briefly skim through your notes again.

But while review is helpful, cramming last minute is NOT. If at all possible, work ahead so that you won't need to fit all your study into the last day. Cramming overloads your brain with more information than it can process and retain, and your tired mind may struggle to recall even previously learned information when it is overwhelmed with last-minute study. Also, the urgent nature of cramming and the stress placed on your brain contribute to anxiety. You'll be more likely to go to the test feeling unprepared and having trouble thinking clearly.

So don't cram, and don't stay up late before the test, even just to review your notes at a leisurely pace. Your brain needs rest more than it needs to go over the information again. In fact, plan to finish your studies by noon or early afternoon the day before the test. Give your brain the rest of the day to relax or focus on other things, and get a good night's sleep. Then you will be fresh for the test and better able to recall what you've studied.

Step 6: Take a Practice Test

Many courses offer sample tests, either online or in the study materials. This is an excellent resource to check whether you have mastered the material, as well as to prepare for the test format and environment.

Check the test format ahead of time: the number of questions, the type (multiple choice, free response, etc.), and the time limit. Then create a plan for working through them. For example, if you have 30 minutes to take a 60-question test, your limit is 30 seconds per question. Spend less time on the questions you know well so that you can take more time on the difficult ones.

If you have time to take several practice tests, take the first one open book, with no time limit. Work through the questions at your own pace and make sure you fully understand them. Gradually work up to taking a test under test conditions: sit at a desk with all study materials put away and set a timer. Pace yourself to make sure you finish the test with time to spare and go back to check your answers if you have time.

After each test, check your answers. On the questions you missed, be sure you understand why you missed them. Did you misread the question (tests can use tricky wording)? Did you forget the information? Or was it something you hadn't learned? Go back and study any shaky areas that the practice tests reveal.

Taking these tests not only helps with your grade, but also aids in combating test anxiety. If you're already used to the test conditions, you're less likely to worry about it, and working through tests until you're scoring well gives you a confidence boost. Go through the practice tests until you feel comfortable, and then you can go into the test knowing that you're ready for it.

Test Tips

On test day, you should be confident, knowing that you've prepared well and are ready to answer the questions. But aside from preparation, there are several test day strategies you can employ to maximize your performance.

First, as stated before, get a good night's sleep the night before the test (and for several nights before that, if possible). Go into the test with a fresh, alert mind rather than staying up late to study.

Try not to change too much about your normal routine on the day of the test. It's important to eat a nutritious breakfast, but if you normally don't eat breakfast at all, consider eating just a protein bar. If you're a coffee drinker, go ahead and have your normal coffee. Just make sure you time it so that the caffeine doesn't wear off right in the middle of your test. Avoid sugary beverages, and drink enough water to stay hydrated but not so much that you need a restroom break 10 minutes into the test. If your test isn't first thing in the morning, consider going for a walk or doing a light workout before the test to get your blood flowing.

Allow yourself enough time to get ready, and leave for the test with plenty of time to spare so you won't have the anxiety of scrambling to arrive in time. Another reason to be early is to select a good seat. It's helpful to sit away from doors and windows, which can be distracting. Find a good seat, get out your supplies, and settle your mind before the test begins.

When the test begins, start by going over the instructions carefully, even if you already know what to expect. Make sure you avoid any careless mistakes by following the directions.

Then begin working through the questions, pacing yourself as you've practiced. If you're not sure on an answer, don't spend too much time on it, and don't let it shake your confidence. Either skip it and come back later, or eliminate as many wrong answers as possible and guess among the remaining ones. Don't dwell on these questions as you continue—put them out of your mind and focus on what lies ahead.

Be sure to read all of the answer choices, even if you're sure the first one is the right answer. Sometimes you'll find a better one if you keep reading. But don't second-guess yourself if you do immediately know the answer. Your gut instinct is usually right. Don't let test anxiety rob you of the information you know.

If you have time at the end of the test (and if the test format allows), go back and review your answers. Be cautious about changing any, since your first instinct tends to be correct, but make sure you didn't misread any of the questions or accidentally mark the wrong answer choice. Look over any you skipped and make an educated guess.

At the end, leave the test feeling confident. You've done your best, so don't waste time worrying about your performance or wishing you could change anything. Instead, celebrate the successful completion of this test. And finally, use this test to learn how to deal with anxiety even better next time.

Review Video: Test Anxiety
Visit mometrix.com/academy and enter code: 100340

Important Qualification

Not all anxiety is created equal. If your test anxiety is causing major issues in your life beyond the classroom or testing center, or if you are experiencing troubling physical symptoms related to your anxiety, it may be a sign of a serious physiological or psychological condition. If this sounds like your situation, we strongly encourage you to seek professional help.

Online Resources

Due to our efforts to try to keep this book to a manageable length, we've created a link that will give you access to all of your online resources:

mometrix.com/resources719/dsstprinpubsp

It's Your Moment, Let's Celebrate It!

Share your story @mometrixtestpreparation